BOOK FIVE

CHANGED LIVES

Ten True Stories: From Addiction to Freedom

Compiled by
PASCO A. MANZO

Foreward by PASTOR GARY WILKERSON

Changed Lives (Book Five)
Ten True Stories: From Addiction to Freedom
Compiled by Pasco A. Manzo

Teen Challenge New England, Inc.
1315 Main Street
Brockton, MA 02301

All Scripture quotations are taken from the Holy Bible, New International Version® unless otherwise noted. NIV®. Copyright © 1973, 1978, 1984 by International Bible Society, Zondervan Bible Publishers.

Edited by Brett Seastedt and Mary Ann Manzo
Jacket and Layout Design by Colton Simmons
and Eric Castonguay

ISBN: 978-0-692-12348-5

Printed in the United States of America
2018 - First Edition

Dedication

This book is dedicated to ... the countless caring, loving, compassionate, benevolent, unselfish, kind, and generous people who believe in the Teen Challenge mission and give considerable time, talent, and treasures again and again to see hopeless addicts find hope, healing, and freedom.
Thank You!

"...the righteous give generously."
Psalm 37:21

Contents

Back Page Contents

Foreword

Pastor Gary Wilkerson

There is a light in the darkness; there is a candle that is inextinguishable. And there is hope when all seems lost—a hope that breaks every bondage. In a world of fallen humanity—where children are abandoned to the streets, where marriages are discarded without a care, where addictions destroy lives and wreak havoc in our communities—we are not left hopeless or helpless. We have a Savior, a Redeemer, a Champion—Jesus Christ, who comes to the rescue of all. Those of us at Teen Challenge know this hope—and, more to the point, we know the Savior—and we offer an answer to the broken and the hurting of this world.

Bringing hope within reach of every addict is the calling of Teen Challenge. And I can tell you, this ministry does it better than anyone else in the world. There is no more wholistic approach to recovering life as God intended it than the approach Teen Challenge takes. It touches the spirit, heals the soul, and restores the body. It makes way for a bright future—igniting the divine spark of life, relighting the candle of the soul, and renewing the mind and body to live to the fullest. Teen Challenge offers the hope of abundant life.

The stories you read here will send chills down your spine and thrills to your heart. It will show you that what seems impossible in a defeated culture is accomplished by God daily through Teen Challenge. I can't say the miraculous is commonplace at this ministry, but it happens regularly. Read this book and share it: Give it to your family and friends, and get extra copies for your church, neighborhood, and community. It offers more than statistics and cold, hard data. It contains the life-changing power of the gospel of Jesus Christ—and the hope that someone needs today. You can support this ministry by praying for them daily and by getting the Good News contained here to those who need it.

With the current epidemic of opioids taking the lives of thousands, we stand in need of a reliable and robust remedy. When my father, David Wilkerson, first started Teen Challenge, he had no idea that decades later there would be over 1,400 centers worldwide with nearly 20,000 people being cared for at any given time. Yes, right now, 20,000 people are being set free from life-destroying bondages of addiction. Teen Challenge New England & New Jersey is on the cutting edge of a move of God to stem the rising tide of life-controlling problems; they do it well. Lives are changed, families are restored, communities find there is an answer to addiction. Hope is found at Teen Challenge, a hope that rests fully on Jesus Christ.

Introduction: Christian Twelve Step Recovery Guide

Scott O'Neil

Many of us are familiar with the twelve step program of Alcoholics Anonymous. Founded in 1935 by Bill Wilson and Dr. Bob Smith, AA is spiritually based program where recovering alcoholics help each other stay sober. While it is spiritually-based, it uses general terms like "god" and "higher power" so that person can choose their own faith. They wanted to appeal to a wider audience and ultimately help more people get sober.

Christian-based twelve step groups, such as Celebrate Recovery founded by Pastors John Baker and Rick Warren, is singular in faith, following the teachings of the Bible and stating that Jesus Christ is the only God. Below is a guide to the Christian twelve steps.

Christian Twelve Step Recovery Guide

Step One: **We admitted we were powerless over**

our separation from God – that our lives had become unmanageable.

Scripture: *"For I know that good itself does not dwell in me, that is, in my sinful nature. For I have the desire to do what is good, but I cannot carry it out."* Romans 7:18 (NIV)

As an addict who wants to become victorious over their addiction, you must first recognize the issue and ask yourself some very important questions – you owe it to yourself. Can you cope with the reality of past hurts or future fears without using some sort of substance? Can you enjoy getting together with friends or family without substance? If a desire triggers within you, can you wholeheartedly say that you have the power to refrain from it? If not, then chances are you have a problem that won't go away until you recognize it.

Identifying that we are not in the best standing with God, we must look into why that is, and require that He take control. Admitting that we have fallen short of the standards that both God and ourselves expect is the first step we need in order to go down the right path. Without this, we are still swimming in our own pool of addictive habits and character that will, without question, lead us back to active addiction.

Step Two: **We came to believe that a Power greater than ourselves could restore us to sanity.**

Scripture: *"For it is God who works in you to will and to act in order to fulfill his good purpose."* Philippians 2:13 (NIV)

How can one find hope in something if they do not believe? To break the normalcy of our dependency, we must depend on something different, something greater than ourselves. The blessing of knowing God and forming a relationship with Jesus Christ is that He will restore your thinking and help to sharpen a mind that has been destroyed through the use of drugs and alcohol. But the question will remain: do you believe that God is whom He claims to be? And if so, do you trust Him with your life to find sanity and a healthy lifestyle?

Restoration of sanity isn't confined to thinking. Restoration of sanity includes a healthy emotional state as well. God will give you the tools you need to fight anxiety and many other things that try to conquer our soul, spirit, and body. Drug addiction brings a sense of identity to it. People have begun to call you a "junkie," "addict," or "severe alcoholic." God wants to restore you, bring healing, and to call you His child. A new identity of who you are in relation to God brings a new facet of healing to the addict seeking recovery.

Step Three: **We made a decision to turn our will and our lives over to the care of God, as we understood Him.** Scripture: *"Therefore, I urge you, brothers and sisters, in view of God's mercy, to offer your bodies as a living sacrifice, holy and pleasing to God – this is your true and proper worship."* Romans 12:1 (NIV)

Changed Lives

Surrendering to God is the most freeing decision you can ever make. We must realize that during our time in addiction, we were constantly surrendering to our desires to get high. If we seek to surrender to God and depend on Him for strength, then you will have the strength you need to refrain from using drugs or alcohol. This decision is the most important one that you can make in your entire life and it is worthy of heavy consideration.

This step will take some discipline. As an addict, your every moment is incessantly seeking a way to get high. Not by the mind alone, but by the physical withdrawals of the drugs and alcohol that have taken your body captive. It's going to be the most difficult during the first few months of surrender. You must be intentional about thinking about Jesus, staying in prayer, and not letting the thoughts of getting high overcome you. Bring your weaknesses before Him and let Him work in you.

Step Four: **We made a searching and fearless moral inventory of ourselves.**

Scripture: *"Let us examine our ways and test them, and let us return to the LORD."* Lamentations 3:40 (NIV)

This is one of the most painful parts of the process. Understand that this pain is necessary and is the beginning of the healing from the things you may have gone through or done to others. Humans are, because of our sinful nature, selfish. An addict is even more so, for what we care most about is ourselves, feeling good, and not feeling emotional or physical pain. Our addiction has inflicted pain on numerous people, most often those we love and who love us the most.

By searching our moral failures and lamenting over them, we learn the path that led to our current destruction, but we must be objective and we must be honest if we want the fullness of healing. Do not sugar-coat the wrongs you have done to others, understand the impact and with the pain will come a desire, a desire to never want to partake of those things ever again.

Just as a disclosure, you will not have to stay in this mourning forever, but you must go through it to understand the ugliness of addiction. Then when desires arise you associate that desire with the moral failures and the addiction you are embarking to leave behind.

Step Five: **We admitted to God, to ourselves, and to another human being the exact nature of our wrongs.** Scripture: "Therefore confess your sins to each other and pray for each other so that you may be healed. The prayer of a righteous person is powerful and effective." Romans 12:1 (NIV)

Can you see how the other steps flow into this one? By believing, searching, and now admitting, you are taking a crucial role in removing the stains of drug addiction from your life. By admitting and confessing to God Himself, you are acting by faith that the God whom you cannot see is hearing your prayers and the start of a wonderful relationship that you will never regret has begun.

The Bible teaches that when we confess our sin there is a healing that comes from that action. By hiding our wrongs, we place an unnecessary burden upon ourselves and upon others that weighs on our conscience. Allow the truth to be revealed and though initial pain may accompany it, you will realize that there is a sense of freedom.

By talking about it with others, you might be able to get good perception of what happened, and what you need to do to stay the course. Other people might be able to bestow wisdom of why you ended up where you were. If not, it's a good practice to be accountable to others, especially the people you love and who want to see you be successful.

Step Six: **We were entirely ready to have God remove all these defects of character.**

Scripture: *"Humble yourselves before the Lord, and he will lift you up."* James 4:10 (NIV)

Sometimes we find ourselves in such a great conflict that we need to search deeper about ourselves. We are dishonest about who we are; there is something inside us that wants to project a certain image towards others that may even be self-deceptive. We may have the pride of being a "rebel," maybe the "craziest" amongst our peers. We must want to shake the hardness that has come from years of rejection and making poor decisions. Does this sound like you? Do you have the tendency to want to be combative and not surrender?

After years of watching people fail and succeed I've noticed one thing about people who fail: They are unwilling to allow God to work in the protected areas of their heart. They still want to project as the outlaw, the one who stands down to no one and does their own thing. But it's this kind of attitude that helped contribute to your demise.

Make yourself ready to change. Weigh everything on the table and look at the many people who have gone through recovery and ask yourself, "Is this what I want in life?" If you are not yet ready, continue the pros and cons of using drugs and not using drugs. Think about what kind of life and legacy you want to leave behind. God's path is very admirable and honorable.

Step Seven: **We humbly asked Him to remove our shortcomings.**

Scripture: *"If we confess our sins, he is faithful and just and will forgive us our sins and cleanse us from all unrighteousness."* 1 John 1:9 (NIV)

It's time to take the next step and ask God to remove these character defects. Just so you know, this is not going to be easy by any means. It's kind of like an infected tooth, the process is painful but when the infection is removed you are much better off. God is good at taking out the infections of addiction and cleaning up your character.

As you go through this stage you will have to constantly be in a state of surrender to His work inside you. He will lead you and begin to take out unhealthy desires that lead to your destruction. One must take a step in denying themselves to allow the desires that control us to pass. You may fail many times, but remember that little progress is better than no progress or remaining in the same state that you are in. It would be far worse to remain where you are than to strive to what lies ahead in this journey.

Step Eight: **We made a list of all persons we had harmed and became willing to make amends to them all.** Scripture: *"Do to others as you would have them do to you."* Luke 6:31 (NIV)

This step brings a very sobering reality to the previous steps and starts to make everything so much more real. By this I mean that you now must look into the eyes of the people you wronged and humbly ask for forgiveness. Be aware there might people you wronged that aren't so quick to forgive you. A lot of us were very destructive and hurtful to the family members and friends we were the closest to, and some of the things we have done to them do not go away overnight.

Be thorough in your listing, make sure you cover every

base, but I don't recommend much time spent on drug buddies. Also, if you were in some shady business with people, it's not a good idea to go out and seek their forgiveness, as it would not be healthy for either party involved.

Step Nine: **We made direct amends to such people wherever possible, except when to do so would injure them or others.**

Scripture: *"Therefore, if you are offering your gift at the altar and there remember that your brother or sister has something against you, leave your gift there in front of the altar. First go and be reconciled to them; then come and offer your gift."* Matthew 5:23-24 (NIV)

"Wherever possible" is a very important part of this step. Sometimes we get so zealous in getting forgiveness from people that we end up hurting ourselves. Some things are better off letting go of rather than pursuing an unhealthy relationship that you know might cause more damage to your recovery process.

Step Ten: **We continue to take personal inventory and when we were wrong promptly admitted it.**

Scripture: *"So, if you think you are standing firm, be careful that you don't fall!"* 1 Corinthians 10:12 (NIV)

Continuing to take personal inventory is a lifelong journey that will aid your character for the rest of your life. There is no substitute for reflecting on your life and being willing to improve as a person and to the way God has intended for you to live. One warning that comes from this is to not be prideful, not to think you are above others because you have some "clean time," but constantly through humility take an honest look at yourself.

Step Eleven: **We sought through prayer and meditation to improve our conscious contact with God as we understood Him, praying only for knowledge of His will for us and the power to carry that out.**

Scripture: *"Let the message of Christ dwell among you richly."* Colossians 3:16A (NIV)

We must understand the will of God and this comes from reading the Bible and spending time in prayer with Him. Only by getting to know God will we be able to understand His love, His heart, and His will for our lives. God doesn't want you to remain in bondage anymore and sent His Son so that you may be set free from the burdens that are weighing you down.

When we change our focus from our will to God's will we will become more intentional with our lives and not subject to making rash decisions. Having a selfless ambition to put away our past hurts and mistakes and pursue the future with an open heart to hear God's voice, it becomes easier not to fall into past temptations because our minds are not filled with such thoughts.

Step Twelve: **Having had a spiritual awakening as the result of these steps, we tried to carry this message to others, and to practice these principles in all our affairs.** Scripture: *"Brothers and sisters, if someone is caught in a sin, you who live by the Spirit should restore that person gently. But watch yourselves, or you also may be tempted."* Galatians 6:1 (NIV)

Testifying about your story can be extremely liberating. When you begin to tell your story to others you are, in a sense, dealing with your past and using it as a warning to others. At the same time you are experiencing freedom and being used as a trophy of God's grace.

When you share your message with others you are going through a process of healing and declaration of not being the person you used to be. This could be one of the most powerful ways to help others who are broken, as you once were, and to break the spirit of addiction in their lives.

The Serenity Prayer by Reinhold Niebuhr

God, grant me the serenity, to accept the things I cannot change, the courage to change the things I can, and the wisdom to know the difference. Living one day at a time; accepting hardship as a pathway to peace; taking, as Jesus did, this sinful world as it is; not as I would have it; trusting that You will make all things right if I surrender to Your will; so that I may be reasonably happy in this life and supremely happy with You forever in the next. Amen.

Chapter 1
A Therapist Comes to Teen Challenge

Douglas S. Tubach LMHC M.Div

"Are you still interested in working with us here at Teen Challenge?" I was shocked! This was a message I was reading on my phone. The message continued, "If you are still interested and still doing counseling, call me on my cell." Well I ran out of my office and got to a private place and called the number. Allison Cruz answered and said, "Boy, that was quick." I said, "Hi Allison, I'm not one to play games. Sure I am still interested."

Ever since I heard David Wilkerson preach in Boston, Massachusetts while I was attending Berklee College of Music and heard the book "The Cross and the Switchblade" read to me, I wanted to work for Teen Challenge. But yes, I was going to music school because I loved music and wanted to be in a band like the Beatles and be famous. I had always loved music since I was young. My parents would play beautiful movie soundtracks like "The Music Man," South Pacific," and "My Fair Lady" for my sister and I.

Along with the music in our home, there was a whole lot of love and joy. My parents were wonderful and raised us with Biblical values. One of their most amazing demonstrations of love was how they supported and accepted me even though I was born legally blind. Yep, through no fault of my parents this was something that God planned for my good. My mom was the best and did everything she could to prepare the way for me. My parents even moved into a school district where there was a person who specifically worked with the visually impaired. God also surrounded me with three best friends who were always there for me.

Life was great and I was succeeding. I rose to the top of my class in eighth grade and became Student Council President in the ninth grade. I had my own musical group and not only that, I had my first girlfriend who liked me and I liked her. Life was great! Then it began to change. I messed up my relationship with Lisa by trying to be a tough and cool guy. Then as high school progressed my three best friends all started to go in different directions. That was all very depressing and I didn't know what to do and then that produced anxiety as I would try to figure it all out but couldn't. However, I was determined to pursue my music. I joined a band in high school with the best players in the area. They were definitely better than me. We rehearsed every day and played dances and school events on Friday nights. But I felt horrible. One night I was at a party and I drank three beers and I felt okay again.

> So throughout high school I drank some and started smoking marijuana. This took away my depression and anxiety temporarily.

I also rejected church; nobody was serious enough about their faith to suit me. I had begun to question the Bible and basic beliefs.

When I got to Berklee, I started smoking weed every day. I would go to class and practice five hours and then get high. But I knew I needed to get back with God. I found a group of students that were having a Christian meeting in Berklee's cafeteria and I started to go to the meetings. WOW, the Holy Spirit also was going to those meetings and began to flow through me. A few touches of the Holy Spirit and I knew that I could know Jesus in a personal way and that everything in the Bible was true. So I made Jesus Lord of my life and asked God to show me how to put everything under His Lordship. I wanted to follow what the Bible said about every area of my life. I had always been good at getting up in front of people and speaking and I really felt like I was called to preach, so I started going door to door in the dorms telling people to repent and turn to Jesus. This didn't go so well. I also would stand up in the school cafeteria during supper and start preaching. Waves of vegetables like corn and peas found their way onto my face and jeers from the students echoed in my ears. The worst part of it was that the leader of our college fellowship didn't agree with what I was doing. He had been the one to disciple me, and he had been everything I thought a Christian should be. He was in the process of walking away from Jesus and I couldn't believe what was happening. Things got to the point that he called the ambulance because he thought there was something drastically wrong with me. So I was taken to the hospital and was under observation for two and a half weeks and then released.

Broken and crushed I went home to my parents, leaving in the middle of my fourth semester, feeling like a complete failure. I spent the next nine months going through a severe crisis of faith, questioning God, doubting my own salvation, and believing that I must not be chosen by God after all. But my mom showed the love of Jesus beyond measure and never doubted God's plan for me, for she would quote Philippians 1:6 over and over. "He that has begun a good work in you will bring it to completion to the Day of Jesus Christ." She wouldn't stop encouraging me that God was going to use this trial to prepare me and train me to help others one day. This was part of the preparation for me ultimately working at Teen Challenge. Clearly I had moved ahead of God's timing for me. I was NOT ready to preach publicly and to reach out the way I did. I did go back to Berklee and finished my Bachelor's Degree and played in a few Christian bands. It was the following year that I heard David Wilkerson preach in Boston right around the corner from Berklee. Seven years later I moved to New York and got trained by Don Wilkerson and Pastor Jimmy Lilley. It was the year right before Times Square Church began. I also had an opportunity to be David Wilkerson's son Gary's prayer support at the church. But I was not spiritually ready for all that that would entail.

All my dreams came crashing down on me. The girl I thought God had for me to marry married someone else despite all my efforts to stop her (this was the girl who read The Cross and the Switchblade to me). Then the Lord made it clear that my other dream of making it in music was not His will. Although I had been meeting with the man who had first booked the Beatles here in America at Carnegie Hall and promoted and managed a number of major acts and he was beginning to help me, one day I distinctly sensed that the Lord was telling me to stop pursuing music.

Both disappointments were devastating. I spent the next five years healing from the loss of these two big dreams.

The Holy Spirit, who is the Perfect Counselor, did intensive therapy with me during those five years.

He knows how to help someone who has experienced huge losses and is grieving those losses. He used a combination of healing strategies including solitude, stillness, rest, reflection, and the deep work of counseling me about accepting God's will, not my own and waiting on Him.

After going back to my home in Nebraska for two of those five years, the Holy Spirit began to gently and tenderly move on me to consider going to seminary. Miraculously, a large sum of money came to me that enabled me to pay for both a Master of Divinity Degree and a Master of Arts in Counseling. The Lord also brought to me the woman that He had picked for me to marry. So I left seminary with two degrees and one wife.

I worked at Boston Rescue Mission for two years, got licensed as a mental health counselor, and then practiced for 13 years in a Christian counseling center. Through all of this, I still I had a deep sense that God had called me to work at Teen Challenge. So when I got that phone call from Allison I began to see my dream come true.

MY START AT TEEN CHALLENGE

Allison set up an interview with the President of Teen Challenge New England & New Jersey, Pasco Manzo. The interview went well and a few months later I started. When

I first walked into my office and began to pray I immediately felt the manifest presence of the Holy Spirit. Oh, this is so wonderful, I thought. Then I looked around and saw what a big office it was filled with brand new furniture. I felt so amazed and grateful. What are the expectations though? This was clearly something God had brought about. He had proven to me that when I made Jesus Lord of my life that He would be the one to bring about my dreams, not me. Well there I was, sitting in my office with the President's words ringing in my ears.

"Doug, I want you to figure out why some guys who have been through the program are relapsing and I want you to help them."

He also spoke about those who are dual diagnosis cases, which means that along with their drug addiction they have other disorders, such as PTSD, bipolar, depression, anxiety, etc.

Overwhelmed? Yes. But thankfully, in the last few years in my counseling practice I had been discovering marvelous breakthroughs, especially in my couples counseling work. For example, I would be in the middle of a session with a husband and wife and they would have escalated to a fever pitch of argument and I would find myself outside of the conversation. What I would begin to do was call on Jesus silently in my heart and all of a sudden one of them would finally admit their wrongs or apologize or say something heartfelt that would completely turn the tide of the session. Clearly the Holy Spirit was at work. Jesus said that He was the Counselor after all. I was beginning to see that it was about me stepping back and letting the Lord lead the session. I had to give Jesus first place in the therapy, not depend on formula or counseling technique.

FOUNDATIONS OF COUNSELING

Having the ministry of counseling at Teen Challenge is certainly not a new idea. As you read David Wilkerson's early books like, *Twelve Angels from Hell* and *Hey Preach You're Coming Through,* you will find many examples of how he was implementing strategies of counseling with the residents he reached out to. Brother Dave and his brother Don Wilkerson compiled a great primer on counseling for Teen Challenge workers called *The Untapped Generation.* In there you will find instructions on how to counsel people with varied life controlling problems. Brother Dave was an effective counselor. In a sermon I heard him preach at Times Square Church he shared a story of a particular counseling session he had with a woman who had experienced severe and complicated trauma and he did a skilled job at helping her. Then around the year 2000, Minnesota Adult and Teen

Challenge took the next step and began bringing in clinicians to provide counseling and therapy.

MY METHOD

My ministry at Teen Challenge is patterned after what Jesus did while here on earth. He came to heal the brokenhearted. (Luke 4:18) I want to follow Jesus in this. Jesus was in total harmony with both the Father and the Holy Spirit. Jesus only did His Father's will in every situation. The Holy Spirit empowered Him and led Him clearly to each situation and equipped Him with what to say and how to do it. WOW! The combination and blending of the work of the Godhead is powerful. This is a mystery, yet so marvelous! Jesus loved each person perfectly. And in doing so He knew exactly what it was that each person needed to take that next step of growth and healing and what that next step would be. For Nicodemus it was "You must be born again." For another it was "Go sell everything you have and come and follow me." For another it was that Jesus looked at a man and just loved him. Now, I'm not in perfect harmony with the Father's will and am not perfectly attuned to the leading of the Holy Spirit, so I PRAY, "Heavenly Father line me up with Your will, not mine and Holy Spirit cause me to get on board with what You are already doing in this precious person's life so that he may find and take that next step in his healing."

MY STRATEGY

In most sessions I begin with prayer. Acknowledging God first only makes sense. It's all about Jesus ultimately. He is the One that created and established Teen Challenge and He is the One who brought the person here and brought me to counsel them. I find myself in the midst of a divine plan and I must look to the Designer for everything.

I listen, wonder, ask questions, explore, see, and discover possible pathways of healing. Are you really hearing me Doug? I love to listen. Being born legally blind put me in a position where listening was essential to me getting almost anywhere in life.

What someone says is very important, but there is so much more in what they are saying.

I have learned to hear feeling, desire, and deep emotion in the human voice.

I will begin to get a sense about a person's past, their present, and hidden nuances to their personality as I listen. I love people and as I listen it is through that skill that I begin to appreciate the person who has come to see me. God is so creative! Each person is so unique and valuable to God and others. The differences and mysteries in each individual are astounding. To love is to appreciate and as I appreciate this delightful person in front of me, I see the glory of God manifest. So in the midst of this seeing the glory of God I can't help but ask questions.

This must be done with care. Questions are powerful instruments. And if used casually or carelessly there can be damage done and I could further injure the special person that is there with me. I must proceed carefully as I see truth about someone. It is often the case that before I ask a question, I will move into prayer.

As a session unfolds, God is faithful to begin to show either a specific area that needs change or something in particular that needs healing. God's light that shines on these areas is a light of love and compassion. These points of healing are seen and discovered through a connection and bond that God forms between the resident and me, undergirding all of this is for me to be truly present in the moment and to provide a safe emotional and spiritual space for the person to be open honest and vulnerable.

Having a licensed clinician like myself, the laws of confidentiality and privacy are in effect. So the person coming to see me can share without fear of me telling the staff some personal issues that are troubling them. The limits to this are also the same as I am mandated to report if someone is deemed to be a threat to harm self or others. This freedom to share has been received with much gratitude from the residents and often times the guys will thank me for the opportunity to vent and really share what is bothering them without the fear of misunderstanding or reprisal. Many guys have shared with me that I am the only one they have ever been able to tell certain things to. Others have remarked that the sessions are a time when they can truly relax and be themselves.

Conditions of Brokenness - A Brief List

The most talked about problem at Teen Challenge is addiction. That is the condition of most of the guys presently in the program. But many of the guys have at least one if not more other issues that are diagnosable as disorders. Here are a few co-occurring disorders.

Grief, Loss, and Abuse: Many of the guys through no fault of their own have experienced a large amount of loss and grief. Many guys have lost parents at an early age or the parents divorced when they were young. Then there are those who experienced physical and sexual abuse growing up in and out of their families. These guys are experiencing the fallout of Post-Traumatic Stress Disorder. Some of the guys have been on the other side of the abuse and have been the cause of the trauma in others.

Anxiety Disorders: There are those that come into the office who, along with their addictions, have panic disorder, generalized anxiety disorder, and other anxiety conditions. Sometimes it is a result of trauma and other times it is biologically based.

Bipolar Disorder: I have seen a number of guys that suffer with bipolar disorder and they were trying to cope with it through their drug use. This is a tough one because, for one reason, when a person is in a manic phase they usually are very productive, and this is deceptive. One thinks then that they are all right. But when the crash comes and the depression sets in they have disaster awaiting them.

A Unique Case: I had the privilege of working with a man who suffered from sex addiction and alcoholism. He had been a stripper for seven years and had lived the lifestyle that commensurate with these addictions. He didn't feel like he fit in the program and had a struggle with many of the students. He told me how he felt that my office was an oasis and a refuge for him. He also had a great interest and gifting in the performing arts community and had a gift for dance. God had done a great work in his life. He had a genuine love for the Lord and a deep experience in worship. I began to share with him ways to deal with his sex addiction through his relationship with the Lord. He began to find the fulfillment he was looking for as he worshipped the Lord and these experiences were liberating him from his lust.

> He began to see the Lord as the true lover of his soul
> and that he was created to worship the Lord, not his
> own pleasure and women.

Practically speaking as he would think of a woman or when he would see one, he would begin to give praise to God as her Creator and he would thank God for her beauty and find himself caught up in adoration of God and hence find emotional release. He had discovered that God is the giver of pleasure through the beauty of His creation, but for us to stay out of sin, we must give back to Him through worship that pleasure we receive. He knows that the patterns of the past are deep-seated, but he sees that God has provided a pathway for his deliverance. Praise God!!!

Back to President Manzo's original question to me, which was, "I want you to find out why guys who have been through the Program are relapsing?" I have a few answers:

1. Priority Shifts. A number of men in the program who have come back on restoration (A six-month program provided for graduates of recovery programs who relapse) have admitted that the reason they relapsed was that they had left their first love and did not keep Jesus first in their lives. They were trying to live a normal life, not "The Normal Christian Life."

2. Playing the Game. There was a resident I knew that I watched go through the program who was faking it. He was smart enough and strong enough to do all that the program required, but he was lying about the most important part of the program: knowing Jesus. So it wasn't long after graduation that he relapsed. When he came back he admitted all this to me. He has since established a genuine relationship with the Lord.

3. Not Facing the Consequences. Some guys will see the miraculous change that God brings in their lives and others and assume from this that every change that they need to go through will be miraculous and quick. So when they get back with their wife or fiancée and begin to have regular interpersonal issues, they assume that God will divinely intervene. They fail to face the damage they did to this special person and are then unable to deal with the consequences.

4. People Have to Want Change. Not all do. But the good news is that God can put the want to in us for God both works in us to will and to do of His good pleasure.

Healing is always miraculous, but it is not always instantaneous, quick, or at the speed we would prefer. But God always knows what He is doing and does what is right in our lives and He is working it all out for our good.

The guys I get to work with have suffered much and have endured much. Some have been victimized, while others have done the victimizing. Some received genetic weaknesses and predispositions to evil. Some grew up in places no human should ever be. Yet if God can take the greatest evil, which is the death of His own Son, and turn it into the greatest good for everyone, then God can certainly bring healing to the men of Teen Challenge! May His kingdom come and His will be done here at Teen Challenge as it is in heaven.

As you read this chapter and if through Admissions you find yourself coming to the Brockton or Boston Teen Challenge center, there is a good chance I will be your counselor. I look forward to the day we meet and I want you to know there is HOPE for you to experience a changed life!

Chapter 2
No Turning Back

Neil Hooley

I grew up in the suburbs of Cherry Hill, New Jersey, just outside of Philadelphia, with a wonderful family life. My parents were hardworking business owners who sacrificed everything for the benefit of our family. Early on, my brother and I learned first-hand what it meant to be part of the family business and what manual labor and working with our hands meant.

My mother and her family emigrated from Central America in the 1970's, coming from Nicaragua. Being a developing country, she knew experientially what real poverty was. Growing up, my mom always reminded us how blessed we were and always spoke about the faithfulness of God. She reminded us how she grew up with dirt floors and no food for days at a time. She always set the example for us to rely on God for everything, even to this day. I would consider myself "churched" growing up. We attended service Sunday morning at Kingsway Church, another on Sunday night, and one more on Wednesday evening. Later, we added another service on Friday nights for the youth, which continued through my teen years. God was very much a topic of conversation in my home. My family attended church regularly, we participated in all events, outreaches, summer camps, and mission trips. My brother and I were even involved in our youth group worship band.

I would certainly say I knew of God. I had always heard of God and the story of Him sending His only Son Jesus to earth to save the world from sin. This concept and idea I heard a lot, but I never truly understood and accepted it for myself. I lived my life and saw God through the lens of, "I have to earn favor with God in order for Him to love and accept me." I lived life thinking my good deeds would have to outweigh my bad deeds to make it to heaven. I felt like Christianity was just a list of things I couldn't do, which led me to constantly question my faith growing up. Sometimes I would serve God and go to church because I wanted to, but many times I would do it because I was being forced to. I found myself living life with many masks. On Sundays, Wednesday and Friday nights, I would put on my "church" mask. The other days of the week I would put on my "world" mask. At church, around my "church friends," I would act one way, but around my "school friends"

I would act no different than anyone else in the world. Those two lives rarely crossed paths and I got really good at playing those parts.

In high school I began getting involved with the wrong things. I opened the door to drugs and alcohol and soon drugs began to take over my life. It progressed from simply smoking marijuana to a full-on, blown-out pill snorting, coke snorting, and pill popping chase for a high that never got satisfied. I began to have this "garbage disposal" mentality for getting high, where I would take whatever was put in front of me and use it. This was a dangerous place for me. At first I was able to hide it well and balance out every aspect of my life. Certain times of the year I would be so focused on wrestling that I would forget all about using; but as soon as the season was over, I was right back at it again. There was that constant tension of being clean, playing sports, and getting high. As I was nearing graduation, the signs that something was wrong with me were more evident. My actions and attitude showed the negative results of drug use: manipulating everyone, selfish ambitions, stealing, and lying; everything that comes with having to get money for the next high.

After graduating, I figured I'd give college a go, since that was what everyone else was doing. I applied to Bible College and was accepted. I figured that going to a Bible College may help get me back on track, but I quickly learned

45

that no matter what environment you put yourself into, there will always be people looking to do the wrong thing. After a semester of skipping class and wasting my time and money, I returned back home to New Jersey and began to open up to my family about my drug use and needing help. They accepted me and the fact that college maybe wasn't for me. That was a big moment for me, because I always felt like I had to please my parents and everyone else around me and get assurance from them by doing what everyone else says I should do. In that moment, I decided I was going to stop the drugs and start living right for me.

I began to go back to church and God really began to get my attention. I remember having moments alone in my bedroom reading my Bible and God would speak to me right where I was in life through scripture. The words were jumping off the pages and really making sense to me for the first time ever. I experienced the real presence of the Holy Spirit during my worship and prayer times. For about six months I was on fire for God and clean. I would attend church regularly and serve with the youth. I was even asked to give my testimony and share what God was doing in my life on Easter Sunday at my church. That was the longest I had been clean in a while.

As I stayed clean I began to become healthy again and picked up activities that I once did. One particular day I was on my BMX bike at the outdoor skate park and I fell off my bike and injured my back. I walked out of the emergency room with a prescription for pain medication which opened the door to feeling high again. At this time, I began to receive random phone calls from old friends offering free drugs. The enemy had me right back where he wanted me. This began a six-month downward spiral to drug use and I was the worst I had ever been in my life.

I went from a mountain high experience of God and everything being good in life, to the worst place I've ever been. I moved out of my parent's home, my father fired me from the family business, I was selling weed to support my drug use, and was caught up with the wrong crowd. My family and church family knew things were not right with me. One day my parents and Pastor Ray Tate, the lead pastor of our church at the time, came to my apartment and knocked on my door. I remember at that particular moment I was at a very dark place. I had just come off a three day coke binge and the full effects of coming down were in play.

I felt shame, embarrassment, and at the same time I tried to play off in my mind that I didn't have a problem and that I had this all in control.

That was a lie from the devil that I had believed for a long time.

They knocked at my door for a while but I never answered. They ended up leaving me a letter and a book inviting me to hear them out about a way to get help. I arranged with my parents for a meet up. I went to their house and I sat at their kitchen table as they began to tell me I had a problem and needed help. Inside I agreed 100 percent, but on the outside I played it off as if there was nothing wrong and that I indeed did not have a drug problem. They suggested I get help from a program called Teen Challenge. I had heard about this program when they came and sang as a choir at my church. My parents immediately got us all on speaker phone with the program intake corrdinator who began to tell me what the program was all about. I was still resisting and playing the card that I didn't really need a long term program like that. I mean come on; 15 months to complete the program and 21 months to graduate seemed like an eternity. I remember knowing inside I needed help, but on the outside, I had such a hard time admitting this was the case. In that moment, I decided to give Teen Challenge a try. I was so serious about getting help, that I literally slept in my parent's bedroom. I knew I had to stay close to them in order for me to go.

When I woke up in the morning what I feared most happened. I had an attack of fear and anxiety about going into the program and going away, so I ran out of the house and drove my car as fast as I could back to my apartment. I went to my dark room and ignored everyone. Within a day, police officers were at my door asking for the keys to my car saying it had been stolen and was registered under a Mr. Raymond Hooley Sr. "Thanks Dad; that was a real good move." I had to give up my car. Not only was I jobless and addicted, but now I had no form of transportation. After a couple days I went right back to my ways: selling drugs and using drugs. Three days went by and I was in the middle of a drug deal in my apartment. Let's just say things did not go well and I ended up with a gun to my head. I remember in the moment the Holy Spirit speaking to me. Gently and quietly, I felt Him say, "This is your last chance - either you go to Teen Challenge like you were supposed to go three days ago, or you will end up in jail or dead." It was then I knew I had to do everything in my power to get to Teen Challenge.

That hour I called my parents and told them to pick me up and take me to the program. As I walked out of my apartment and got into my parents' car I remember feeling like I was walking from death to life. They drove me to Teen Challenge New Jersey that night and I began my intake. At the time the New Jersey center was in Newark in a rough part of town next to a crack house. I thought to myself, "This is not going to be good." The plan was that I would be transferred to Teen Challenge Brockton the next day. That first night in Teen Challenge, while on a top bunk in my room holding my Bible, I remember asking God to speak to me again. Although I had been ignoring Him and refusing to read my Bible or pray, in that moment I needed Him. As I flipped open my Bible it landed on Isaiah 43:1-3, "But now, O Jacob, listen to the Lord who created you. O Israel, the one who formed you says, "Do not be afraid for I have ransomed you. I have called you by name; you are mine. When you go through deep waters, I will be with you. When you go through rivers of difficulty, you will not drown. When you walk through the fire of oppression, you will not be burned up; the flames will not consume you. For I am the Lord, your God the Holy One of Israel, your Savior." I felt it was not a matter of "IF" this will happen, but "WHEN" this happens and as if God was talking directly to me saying, "This next 15 months are going to be hard, but I am with you.

> When you feel like you're drowning, I am with you. When you feel like the fire is all around you about to consume you, I am with you."

I felt Him encouraging me and saying, "Do not be afraid!"

The next day I was transferred to Teen Challenge Brockton. My first morning in Teen Challenge I woke up at 5:00 AM for morning prayer. I thought I was going to die. They told me we were going to go pray for one hour to start our day. I learned this was part of my next 15 month daily routine. That was a tough pill to swallow. On day three, I wanted to leave and asked if I was able to make my phone call. They fought me on it for a while, but finally they let me make my call. I called my mom, as I always did when I needed help. I remember hearing her voice. It was obvious she was crying and she was fighting with everything within her, but she said NO. I know that was really hard for her. She never said NO to me. My dad then quickly got on the phone and said, "Son, we love you, but if you happen to find your way back to New Jersey you are not welcome here. Either you finish the program or we cannot help you," and then he hung up. So, at that moment I had a decision. Do I somehow figure out where in the country I am and which direction is New Jersey? At this point, there was no such thing as an iPhone or GPS in the palm of your hand. I was in the middle of Brockton, Massachusetts, a pretty rough neighborhood, and did not have a clue what direction to even start. Even if I somehow miraculously made it to New Jersey, I was not allowed to go home.

I believe in that moment I made one of the best of many decisions I ever made in my life. I decided to stay and not leave. The next morning at 5:00 AM were praying, singing songs, and listening to a Bible devotion. That morning was special. Although all the men were singing out of tune and not in sync, they sang from their hearts. As I listened to the words and then slowly began to utter them myself. "I have decided to follow Jesus, I have decided to follow Jesus, I have decided to follow Jesus, no turning back, no turning back." And as we sang these words, tears began to stream down my face, and

Changed Lives

I felt the presence of God so clearly. I continued to sing, "The cross before me the world behind me, the cross before me the world behind me, the cross before me the world behind me, no turning back, no turning back. Though none go with me, still I will follow, though none go with me, still I will follow, though none go with me, still I will follow, no turning back, no turning back." At that moment, I felt such confidence that I wanted to serve Jesus with everything I had! No matter what! Whether people follow me, or think it's cool, or agree with it or not: I knew without a shadow of doubt that I was going to serve Jesus.

It was in that moment that I looked back at my life and realized all the times I would serve God for a little bit, then I would go right back to my old ways and live this "Christianity rollercoaster life" of ups and down of my good deeds versus my bad deeds. But I was missing the point of the Gospel. It has nothing to do with me, but everything to do with Jesus. So all I needed to do was to continue to follow Him and rely on Him and look to Him, even if no one else was.

There was a leader in the program who told me something that I kept throughout the whole program and even to this day. He said, "Don't go through life here one day at a time. Go through life here one moment at a time." He broke down the cliché "One day at a time" to my reality: that every day is made up of a bunch of moments. I could feel good about being in Teen Challenge in the morning, but come lunch time, my mind would begin to drift and the enemy would put crazy thoughts in my head that questioned if I was doing the right thing and was supposed to stay in the program. It's amazing how just a little bit of clean time makes you think all of a sudden you can take over the world and that you have it all together. You start thinking you will do all the things you said you were going to do for all these years. But God knew I needed a long-term program like this just as a stepping stone to what God had for me next.

I told myself, "I will make it to lunch. Then I will make it to dinner." I set goals of 30 days, three months, six months, and when I would reach each goal I was that much more confident of finishing strong. God gave me this word picture to describe what He was doing in my life. I had a foundation in Him, but that foundation had a bunch of cracks in it. He was going to knock the house down and fill in all the cracks in the foundation, and rebuild a new house that could not be shaken. As a resident in the program, we were required to participate in learning center, which consisted of 523 scripture memorizations and 49 character qualities that all needed to be memorized in order to finish the program. Reading about the things of God seemed so elementary to me. Who is God? What is the Trinity? My pride told me that I knew all I needed to know about God, but God reminded me I needed all those cracks to be filled and we were going to start from the beginning.

Throughout the next 15 months, God did just that, bringing me back to the most basic and simplest of truths about Him. He showed me what unconditional love was. I followed the program living moment by moment and allowed God to speak to me through every situation and through every leader. I learned quickly that Teen Challenge was God's program. He moved leaders around as He saw fit. Residents often questioned why God would have a particular person in leadership, but it was those very leaders that God used to speak into my life. I learned that drugs were just the surface of my issues. My underlying issues were much deeper than drug use.

I had to deal with my pride. I learned how to submit to authority even when everything in me did not want to.

It was my underlying issues that led me to use drugs.

In the program, I was a part of the Drug Awareness Team. DAT meant standing in front of a Wal-Mart in 20 degree weather telling everyone in sight about the dangers of drugs and alcohol. This is where God taught me the importance of integrity: doing the right thing even when no one was looking. It was there He taught me the importance of the "One." We would stand for hours and talk to thousands of people. Many times I would think to myself, "How is this helping anyone?" I would be reminded that it took talking to thousands for that one person to hear about a place where they can get help. More importantly, about a God who can make all things new! He can make you a new person. The old life is gone; the new life has come!

Sometimes we would bring someone right off the street back to the center to get help. It was in front of a store where God taught me how to encourage that mom and dad whose son or daughter was struggling with addiction. I realized my story mattered and God wanted to use what I thought was a bad situation of drug addiction for good: to bring hope to families who have someone struggling with addiction.

I first began to feel a call to serve Jesus through ministry while in the program. At the time I had no idea what that would look like. All I knew is that I would take all opportunities put before me. Any door I felt He opened I would walk through, any doors He closed I knew He didn't want. In the program I felt a call to further my education in scripture and seek the credentialing process to become a minister. Even throughout that time, I really didn't know what that would look like. All I knew was that I wanted to give my life to helping tell people about the good news of Jesus. When I finished the 15 months, I knew I had to finish the six month internship and graduate the 21 months! Throughout those six months, God continued to deepen my faith with Him and opened opportunities of leadership throughout the ministry of the Teen Challenge.

After graduating the program, I was hired on as a staff member of Teen Challenge and worked under Pastor Jonathan Mello on our Drug Awareness Team. As a staff member, God continued to deepen my relationship with Him and used every situation good or bad, easy or tough, for growth. At one point during my ministry at Teen Challenge I asked God what He had next for me. Was I called to Teen Challenge forever? Was I to go out and start a church? Was I to become a missionary and travel the world? Who was going to be my wife? Would I have a family or a house? Where will I live? Yet with all these valid thoughts and concerns on my mind, I had such confidence that God had everything under control and His timing was perfect.

The process of Teen Challenge and the work of the Holy Spirit really helped me with patience and fear. If God got me to this point, didn't allow me to die or go to jail, and carried me through the program, He must really have a plan for me. It was those thoughts that kept me confident and going. One summer, I had an opportunity to travel on a mission trip for two months to Central America. It was 2012 and I had been part of the ministry of Teen Challenge since 2007. I used this time to give up my life even more than before to serve Jesus, to seek and search, and wrestle with God on what He had next for my life. I was ready for God to speak and willing to stay at Teen Challenge, work at a local church, go on the mission field, or whatever He had for me.

During my time in Central America, my faith was strengthened but I never really felt God calling me to any direction throughout the trip until my very last week there.

Again, I believe God's timing is always perfect and nothing is by coincidence. We serve a God who is very intentional in everything He does.

The last week on this trip, it "just so happened" that my home church, Kingsway Church, had just arrived in the country and was partnering with the same organization I was with. I saw some familiar faces and to caught up with my old youth pastor Bryon White. Pastor Bryon had just transitioned from youth pastor to the lead pastor. I was able to hear the vision, mission, and passion Pastor Bryon had for our community through Kingsway Church. Things started to become clear. I heard the idea of a church that helps people find and follow Jesus, period! Before the end of the trip, Pastor Bryon pulled me aside and offered me an opportunity to join him with the vision God has put on his heart for our church. I left the trip thinking, is it possible that God would bring me full circle and have me serve at my home church? That idea had not even occurred to me, but God knew! Over the next three months I wrestled with my decision, prayed, and received counsel from several people I looked up to. Everything pointed to walking through this door God had opened and to serve to the best of my ability. My five-year journey through Teen Challenge prepared me for what God had next.

I thought I was going into a 15 month program that would help get me off drugs. I thought I was a helpless drug addict who had nowhere else to go. But God, He had different plans! He used what looked like a very hopeless, broken, bad situation for good! To bring Jesus glory! In 2012 I transitioned from my position in Teen Challenge back to my home church, Kingsway Church in New Jersey. Kingsway Church had been so much a part of my life, so instrumental in me knowing God; it was through this church that some of my best relationships were formed. And God brought me back to serve the church that served me.

To this day, I have boxes of letters of encouragement and hope to keep on going that I had received from this church throughout my time in Teen Challenge! God used all the situations and growth in Teen Challenge to prepare me for my next responsibilities at Kingsway Church. Since my return to Kingsway, God brought into my life my amazing wife, Mindy, after years of longing and praying! God has since blessed us with two beautiful girls, Lily and Esther, and we currently have one more on the way! I've had the opportunity to see our church grow from 150 people to over 1,200 people every weekend throughout four campuses. My family and I have the honor of being sent out as our first Campus Pastors and launching our first Kingsway Church campus in Glassboro, New Jersey. Only God can do something like this! To use someone who seemed to be the least likely of them all to be part of a movement of God in reaching New Jersey for Jesus. We continue to be in awe that we get to play a small part in what God is doing in His church and I believe the best is yet to come! As I look back at the story of my life at this point, my faith is strengthened! I go through life now with such a confidence. God did it for me and He can do it for you!

Chapter 3
From Prison to Program to Pastor

Marçal DaCunha

    I was born in Harare, Zimbabwe, a small, beautiful country in Southern Africa that was known for being a cultural melting pot. I was raised in a Christian home and lived in a big, gated house with maids and gardeners. I grew up with two older sisters and great parents. I went to Sunday school every week and attended an all-boy private school with the uniform and everything. My Dad was a hard-working photographer and had a very successful studio in the city. Every year, he would travel to America to work on our citizenship so that we could migrate to the states one day. Because of his frequent travels, my mother and I were very close. In 1998 the politics in Zimbabwe turned for the worse and a lot of people began to flee the country. Fortunately, because my father had already begun our emigration process to the United States, we were able to move to America almost immediately. My oldest sister

Changed Lives

Renee had recently married and moved to South Africa to start her family and decided to stay behind. Leaving everything we knew, my parents, my sister Simone, and I packed up our lives to start a new chapter in the "Land of the free, and home of the brave." Simone graduated from high school before leaving Zimbabwe and once we were finally in the states, enrolled into Valley Forge Christian College. With limited resources, my parents and I moved into a one bedroom apartment in East Brunswick, New Jersey. We were starting life all over.

I was thirteen years old and all that mattered to me at that age was trying to fit in. I stood out like a sore thumb! I wore clothes that didn't fit, I had a thick accent, I didn't understand the educational system, and I felt very lost. Thirteen is a very vulnerable age and my highest priority was to figure out who I should be to make friends and be accepted. Desperate for direction, I learned who to be through the shows I watched on TV and the music I listened to. Before long, the person I was becoming was not who I was raised to be, and definitely not who God created me to be. It didn't take too long for my behavior to get me into trouble. I had only been living in America for a few months before my first run in with the law. I began to enjoy the rebellious image that was idolized by the kids in my neighborhood and this attention fueled my rebellion even more. There was a sense of excitement every time I was brought home by the police for various menial crimes. The crimes weren't severe, and the consequences didn't create an incentive for me to change, so I didn't. Little did I know, the consequences of my actions would accumulate and the record I was making for myself would later haunt me.

My first taste of reality was at fourteen years old when I went to jail for the first time. I arrived at the County Juvenile Detention Center in the early hours of the morning. I'll never forget how I felt my first night there. The lights were dim, the inmates were sleeping, and the guards towered over me as they firmly gripped my handcuffed arms while walking me down the sterile hallways. The scent of the facility and the echo of metal doors slamming and mechanically locking terrified me. On the outside I was stone-faced, but on the inside, I was a little boy crying out to be back with my parents again. All I could think about was how heartbroken they must have been. I hadn't seen them since that morning when I rushed out the door not knowing how the night would end.

> When I finally made it to my concrete cell and I heard the footsteps grow distant, the tough façade cracked.

I cried a new cry that I never had before. As the tears puddled on my plastic mattress all I could do was think about home. I couldn't believe what I was putting my parents through. My Dad had worked so hard and my parents had sacrificed so much to bring us to the land of opportunity. I was sure they were crying a new cry also, helpless to rescue their little boy.

Four days later I was released after being sentenced

to six months of house arrest and two years of probation. I was so excited to be free again. My intentions were to change my life, excel at school, and be close with my family the way I planned and promised God during my foxhole prayers. It didn't take long for my young mind to get distracted from those very real intentions. My juvenile detention experience had only magnified the bad boy image I had been developing amongst my friends. Soon after my house arrest was lifted, I found myself getting into trouble in the neighborhood again on a regular basis. Throughout my teenage years I was getting arrested so frequently that by the time I was seventeen, I had reached a tipping point. I was charged with five felony counts of possession of weapons as an adult and sentenced to real jail time.

The goals of correctional facilities are retribution, deterrence, incapacitation, and rehabilitation. Throughout my time in jail I was able to progress through high school and participate in some beneficial behavioral programs that have left a positive effect on me to this day. The problem, however, was the inevitable social conditioning that took place constantly amongst the inmates. I learned more about the world that jail tried to keep me away from than I did in the suburban neighborhoods I grew up in. I heard stories about drugs I had never tried or even knew existed. I learned about places I could go to get these drugs so cheap that if I sold them I could make more money than working a regular job.

I was released from jail a few weeks before my eighteenth birthday a different person. I had difficulties finding a decent job with my criminal record and felt the pressure of living up to the reputation I had created for myself. I embraced a victim mentality so that I could rationalize my poor choices. The Bible speaks about this type of spiritual cognitive dissonance, it says, *"In their wickedness, they suppress the truth."* Romans 1:18. Any moral consciousness left in me was challenged by a desire to believe lies about myself so that I could justify my bad decisions. I was excited to try these new drugs and go to the places I had heard about while in jail. My desire to stay out of trouble was eclipsed by a distorted perspective of my priorities. I hit the ground running in the wrong direction and continued to further my criminal reputation. I made decisions that made me become the person I thought I wanted to be. I took many trips to New York to buy ecstasy pills, marijuana, cocaine, and any other drugs I could get my hands on. In less than a year, I grew from a teenager with the potential to do anything I put my mind to, to a full-blown criminal drug dealer.

Throughout my teenage life I had remained on probation and my adult life was starting under the same conditions. It wasn't long before my probation officer started to sense the direction I was heading in. Although I remained under the radar for the harder drugs I was doing, I would repetitively fail my weekly drug tests for marijuana. I'll never forget my probation officer, John, who genuinely tried to redirect me.

Changed Lives

After the consistent evidence that I wasn't doing anything to change my destructive lifestyle, my probation officer decided to send me to a 28-day inpatient drug program. Any form of rehab was the last thing on my mind. I told the counselors everything they wanted to hear so they would release me without delay. After only two weeks, I convinced them that all I did was smoke some pot on occasion, so they recommended I be discharged with outpatient counseling. Since my probation officer was aware that my drug use was more than casual, he saw right through my deception and ordered me to check into a long-term inpatient program.

This began a long journey through the rehabilitation system. I went through eight different drug programs.

Over a seven-year period I spent four and half of those years in jail or in a rehabilitation center.

I met a lot of different people who introduced me to even more drugs and connections than ever before. In the shadows of these places, I saw a darkness in life that most people would never imagine existed. Some of the worst things I've seen happen in my life took place during my time in rehab centers. During this period, I saw almost every drug used in almost every method you could use it. In a halfway house in Pennsylvania, I tried acid and heroin for the first time. I saw people shoot heroin into their feet to hide marks, people lose their minds after one hit on a crack pipe, people overdose, and things too painful to even mention.

After so many years of living a meaningless empty life, I desperately wanted to change. I would see people my age moving forward in life, getting married, and starting families. I resented not knowing what it was like to be happy, smile, or laugh with friends and family. I hated my reflection. When I looked in the mirror I saw a pale, bony, and aged looking face from the years of malnutrition and effect drugs had on my body. I would think about the "old heads" I met in jail and rehab who had spent their entire lives in institutions. They'd tell me, "Get it while you're young so that you don't end up like me," meanwhile that destiny was clearly where I was headed. The reality I created for myself was too painful to accept. Drugs weren't a form of pleasure anymore they became my coping mechanism. I needed to get high to numb the pain and escape reality, but by then it came to a point where my high wouldn't last long enough. I was so tired of spending every moment of every day, from the time I opened my eyes to the time I passed out, trying to obliterate my mind. All I could do was lie to myself to survive. I told myself that these were just the cards I was dealt in life; no one knows what it's like to be the typical immigrant, high school dropout, and manic depressed drug addict. If I can't get a job because of my record and I can't function socially then the only way I can survive is to keep going in the wrong direction. I dived into an even darker life of drugs, carelessness, and destruction.

Changed Lives

I gave up on trying to keep my head above water and chose to sink as deep as I could. I didn't care about probation or attempting to better my life. I resented that the two years of probation I was sentenced to when I was fourteen had turned into thirteen years. I believed that I had spent half of my life trapped in a system that was designed for me to fail. I ignored that it was my own fault for squandering all the opportunities I was given. I had reached a point of no return and I didn't care.

At the lowest point of my life, God began to intervene in a very uncomfortable way. It's no mere coincidence that these series of events took place during the same week that my mother and her church were praying and fasting for me. In one week, I lost everything I had, my parents' house was raided, and I was kicked out from their home. Homeless and abandoned, I felt the only option left was suicide. I took every drug I had in my possession in hopes it would end my life. I consumed thirty-one Xanax pills one by one until they were all gone. The next day when I woke up, my body was in excruciating pain. I felt relieved that I was still alive, but frustrated and scared about literally having nothing left. I realized my life was spared for a reason and I took this second chance to get my life back on track. By now I was a wanted man and I knew my time on the run had earned some jail time. I was ready and willing to face the music.

I asked my father to take me to see my probation officer so I could turn myself in. He had not taken me to probation since I was a teenager and barely knew anything about the life I had lived as an adult. On my way to probation, he asked if we could stop at his church to pray with his pastor. I agreed because I was hoping that God would get me out of the trouble I was in. When I met Pastor Dan Correa, he talked to me about going to a program called Teen Challenge. He had no idea that for the past seven years my parents constantly tried convincing me to go to Teen Challenge instead of all the other programs I went to. I resented Teen Challenge because it was faith based and fifteen months long. I hated that I couldn't have a girlfriend while in the program and I couldn't smoke cigarettes either. I told Pastor Dan I had been to eight other programs in my past without any success. He clearly saw that my mind was made up and simply began to pray for God to have His will in my life. Afterwards, I went to see my probation officer and he was ready with my violation papers. He looked at me with so much frustration because of how careless I was. He truly wanted to help me change, but could see that I was a lost cause. After thirty minutes of going back and forth, he looked at me and said, "Against my better judgment, I've recently been told about a program called Teen Challenge and I'm willing to give you one last chance if you agree to go there." He said, "Either get yourself in Teen Challenge by tomorrow or turn yourself in and go to prison." I couldn't believe what I was hearing. I had made it clear that Teen Challenge wasn't an option, yet it seemed as if everyone was pressuring me to go.

> I ended our discussion, stood up, and told my probation officer, "I'll see you in prison."

I walked out to the parking lot where my dad was waiting and told him about my decision to go to prison. He said he wanted to talk to my probation officer and I agreed, hoping that he could convince my probation officer to give me a better arrangement. As I stood in that parking lot waiting for my dad, smoking cigarettes back to back, a peace came over me that I couldn't understand. I heard a voice saying to me, "You'll only be twenty-four by the time you leave Teen Challenge. It doesn't matter who you've been for these past seven years. These past seven years won't define who you can be for the next fifty years of your life." Within a moment my heart was changed. As my dad came towards the car, before he could even tell me about his discussion with my probation officer, I told him, "I want to go to Teen Challenge." With tears in his eyes, he said, "Your probation officer wanted you to go to Teen Challenge, but said you'd never go." I put my hand on his shoulder, looked him in the eyes, and said, "Believe in the power of the Holy Spirit." Little did my father know, the Holy Spirit had already begun His work on me in the parking lot, during their conversation. It was my father's faith, my mother's prayers, their church fasting, and God's amazing grace that led to the moment where I could say yes and yield to the Holy

Spirit.

The next day I went to Teen Challenge in Newark, New Jersey. From the moment I walked through the doors I was committed to be a Christian, even though I didn't know what that truly meant. I remember the first night I was there lying on the top bunk bed in a room with ten men. That night I prayed to God sincerely for the first time ever. I prayed, "I don't know if You're real and I feel crazy even talking to You right now, but I want to believe. I don't want to believe because other people have told me about You, I'll believe if You show me who You are." Every day I would read my Bible and follow the curriculum, eager to learn more about God. Every Sunday we would go to the Vailsburg Assembly of God church for service and I would listen intently. Three months later, on Easter Sunday in 2008, Pastor Jermel Mayo preached a message entitled *The Three Truths of the Cross.* I had heard the gospel preached prior to this day, but this time was different, this time my heart heard it. In an instant everything made sense and I realized that God was more real than I could have ever imagined. I ran to the altar at the end of that sermon with tears pouring down my face as I fell to my knees and cried out to God. At that altar, in a matter of seconds, God answered every question my skeptical mind held against Him. The Holy Spirit came upon me and at the speed of thought began revealing who God was and is, and who I am and could be. I was crying and said to God, "Why did it take all these years for me to know You are real? Why couldn't I see who You were before I destroyed my life? Why did my sister know You at such a young age, but not me?" Then I heard His still small voice reply, "I didn't make you go through what you went through, you went through what you went through because of the choices you made without Me, but I can take everything you've been through and use you to reach people that your sister can't. I can restore your life for you, if you give your life to Me." I replied, "I'm supposed to be dead right now, but You've kept me alive, so I'll give You my life to use any way You want."

God was faithful to His promise and gave me more than I could have asked or hoped for. There was no way that I could have changed myself. My past history taught me that even my best intentions quickly fade, and bad decisions become my default. Jesus took me as I was and made me someone completely new.

> I became a new creation in Christ, born again, and given a chance I don't deserve, the chance to start life over.

Though my sins were like scarlet He made me white as wool. I understand what the Apostle Paul was saying when he said, *"Christ Jesus came into the world to save sinners—of whom I am the worst. But for that very reason I was shown mercy so that in me, the worst of sinners, Christ Jesus might display His immense patience as an example for those who would believe in Him and receive eternal life."* 1 Timothy 1:15-16.

Teen Challenge is not your average rehabilitation program; it is so much more than that. Teen Challenge is like a spiritual ICU for people who are in critical condition and need to experience supernatural healing in order to live a strong and healthy life. This healing comes from the throne of Christ. Teen Challenge created an environment where I was saturated by the love and power of God, so that I could overcome addiction, and come alive to the purposes He created me for. There were times where I reached breaking points and thought I wouldn't make it, but God allowed me to reach those breaking points to expose areas that He could change and rebuild even stronger and better than before. I'll never forget the advice that kept me from leaving the program when I wanted to give up. "No matter how you feel, keep the commitment that you made to God when you walked through those doors." I excelled through Teen Challenge and allowed God to expose and convict me of every area that needed change. I was committed to the process God was putting me through, bringing all my convictions to God, and asking Him to help me in every area that could hinder my purpose. Through Teen Challenge, I learned that God has the power and desire to change my life.

I graduated Teen Challenge and had the choice to stay on as staff or create an exit plan that included becoming an intern at a healthy church. I called Pastor Dan who had been supporting me throughout my journey and asked his advice.

He said, "You are like a tree, you can keep growing whether you stay in Teen Challenge or not, as long as you are planted in good soil. Never make a decision out of fear, obligation, or guilt." With Pastor Dan's help, we created an exit plan and I began an internship in ministry in my parents' church. My parents' pastor became my pastor and I began to serve God with my feet planted in good soil. God restored my relationship with my family and gave us an even better relationship than we ever had. The entire church and the pastor's family supported me and gave me a strong spiritual foundation. Pastor Dan's wife, Pastor Nancy, committed me to the worship team where I used my musical talent for the kingdom of God instead of the kingdom of darkness. Pastor Dan's daughter, who played her instrument alongside me, was also truly inspirational and helped me in so many ways. She helped me enroll in Christian college and would constantly talk about the Bible with me. We spent almost every day together serving in the church and going to school. She became my best friend and I was happy to have her in my life. It was inevitable, our friendship grew, we fell in love, and wanted to get married. I had never been truly loved by someone like her before and I didn't deserve to have her in my life. I had lived such a poor life, and I had nothing but baggage and the consequences of my past still affecting me. She still stuck with me through it all, loved me for who I was, and married me.

> God is not only a God of miracles; He also has a sense of humor. It just so happens that my wife Krystal was a police officer in the same town where I once was a criminal.

He put us together for His perfect plan and purpose. You see, God's plan to save my life wasn't just for me, it was because He knew the children we would have one day. The person I was could have destroyed who my children would be before they existed, but God's grace is so merciful, and His love is so unstoppable that He fought to get my attention and lead me to where I needed to be one day. Today we have the most beautiful family with our three children Caleb, Eliana, and Judah. I finally know what it feels like to be happy, smile, and laugh with my family. We serve together as pastors in the same church that once prayed and fasted for me. God has taken my strengths, which were formerly used for destruction, and blessed me with new spiritual gifts to be the Executive Pastor at the Middletown Assembly of God church in New Jersey. My wife and I have also become successful inventors of "The Beach Vault," which has brought our story and the opportunity to testify to the amazing grace and power of God to people all around the world. Our story proclaims that there is no limit to what Christ can do in someone's life. "I am a changed life!"

We pray that our story encourages you, whether you're a parent whose child is as lost as I was, or someone who feels as hopeless as I once did. Turn your eyes to Jesus Christ, who

is the Author and Finisher of your faith. He can rewrite any story and change any person. He can take anyone from the lowest depths to the highest heights, if you have faith and place your life in His hands.

Chapter 4
Dead but Now I'm Alive

Steven Stokes

My entire life, I never believed that I could be loved by anybody and especially not by God. My perception of God was always very superficial, but as my life went on it became very difficult for me to say that there was no God and no purpose to life.

I was born right outside of Boston, Massachusetts and my parents divorced when I was nine years old. It was a complicated breakup and one that affected me, my brother and sister, and my entire family. At the age of nine I remember battling thoughts of suicide and I had moments in my life where I felt like I would be better off dead than have to live with the depression that was beginning to consume me. I began to suffer with severe anxiety and Obsessive Compulsive Disorder that I felt ashamed of because it was beginning to be noticeable and drastically affecting my life. I remember being in school and my anxiety and OCD was out of control and my mind would tell me to do things and it would tell me that if I didn't do what it told me to do, then something bad would happen to my family or to me. I felt crippled and wasn't willing to share this with too many people. I didn't believe anyone was capable of helping me so I battled it on my own for as long as I possibly could.

By the age of thirteen I reached a breaking point with my depression, OCD, and anxiety and I sought medical help. I was put on medication and worked with multiple doctors to get on the right medicine that allowed me to be able to function. When a medicine helped me for a few months and I would begin to feel decent, I would stop taking it. This was a cycle in my life until the first time I drank alcohol at the age of fifteen.

My friend and I skipped school and broke into his parent's liquor cabinet and we drank until we were both blacked out. I knew right then that my life was going to be filled with pain, but I never imagined as a fifteen-year-old boy just how dark my life was about to become. I already hated myself enough and I didn't think that it was possible to hate myself anymore then I already did. This turned out later in life to be as untrue a statement as I've ever conjured up.

I began to mix alcohol with pills to get a better high and when I was 17 I was introduced to Oxycontin. At this time in my life something snapped in me and I began to let out all of the anger that I had held in for 17 years. When I was young I was very shy and reserved and I suppressed a lot of my feelings and just learned how to live with depression. At 17 something very dark happened to me and I was unable to control myself any longer.

Multiple long-term stays in psychiatric hospitals couldn't help the things that were going on inside of my mind.

I couldn't be controlled anymore by anyone and my philosophy was, "I have nothing to lose so there's nothing that anyone could possibly do to me."

I began to get involved in criminal and gang activity, street kids, and racist white groups of friends. I hated anyone who wasn't white, but the irony was that the person that I hated the most was the one that I saw when I looked in the mirror. I began to be abusive to women and got involved in very sick relationships and had no boundaries with the things I would say and do.

My family had enough and was ashamed of the person that I had become. At age 18 I had my first overdose and shortly after I began using heroin. Overdoses became a normal occurrence and monthly I was being rushed to the hospital because I had overdosed. Twelve overdoses and three alcohol poisonings later, I began to have thoughts about God (as I understood God). It had to be more than a coincidence that I was still alive at this point. It wasn't just the overdoses; it was being shot at from five feet away and the bullet missing me by two feet, it was getting jumped by 25 guys in Boston and a knife pulled on me and waking up in a puddle of blood that wasn't mine. The cops told me that whoever this was that got stabbed was no longer living because of the amount of blood that they lost. It could not have been coincidence that multiple suicide attempts were unsuccessful. I drove into a telephone pole at 60 mph and my air bag didn't deploy and I walked away uninjured. One of my overdoses caused me to crash head-on with a police vehicle and kept alive by life support machines.

When I came to, the doctor said that for over an hour my respirations were two per minute. She told me that she has never seen that in her medical career and they were just waiting for me to die. I noticed that the hospital room was completely empty so I asked if they had contacted my family and told them what had happened. The doctor said, "Steven your family has grown used to this and everyone we called said, "This is what he does and this is what he's going to do until he dies.'" I remember lying in that bed being barely alive and the pain that I felt the most severely wasn't physical pain, but it was the pain that I've felt my entire life of having no one and being completely alone. I realized how sad my life really was and deep down I wanted to change, but I had no idea how I was going to do that. I just accepted who I had become, but in the back of my mind, I had strong faith that my life had purpose and that someone or something was watching over me. I didn't know why or who, but it became nearly impossible to deny that I wasn't alone.

When I was 21 years old, I began to live on the streets and in my car and sought shelter in drug houses.

> You know that your life is a mess when people in drug houses don't want you there because you're such a liability to them.

Drug dealers and other people were looking for me, all of my overdoses and unpredictability became too much for everyone. My father took me in and when he found me not breathing on his couch twice, he said, "Steve, I love you, but I will not be able to go on in life if I find you dead on my couch." I went back to living in my car and in abandoned buildings. I got comfortable with this lifestyle and at times it actually seemed quite peaceful. I didn't have to see my family, who I was constantly disappointing, or have to deal with all of the guilt. I didn't have to work or have any responsibilities because I would just steal, do odd jobs, and just get high all day. The best part was that I didn't have to feel anything at all. I could just escape and waste away. I thought that dying on the streets would have been the best case for me. This was the reality that I was expecting to come at any moment and I was at peace with it. I just hoped that I didn't have to feel anything when it finally came.

Every day was a struggle to stay out of trouble and out of danger as I was fighting and involved in crime. I had three assault and possession charges, I was running from the police and missing all of my court cases. At this time, a woman that I barely knew in Boston took me in and showed me compassion. She felt bad for my situation, so she gave me shelter and food and I slept on the floor in her house. I still spent a lot of time at drug houses where I would use heroin, speed, and any other drug that I could get my hands on.

It was at this time that people began to reach out to me. I had a friend named Dave, who I grew up with, who was reaching out to my father. I hadn't seen Dave in over ten years and he had a drug problem that he overcame. I was never one to listen to people's stories of overcoming drug addiction. I knew people did it and can do it, but I just never wanted to. I knew it was much more than my addiction that I was struggling with. I knew that even without drugs, I was the worst person that I knew. I only cared about myself and my mind was so sick and perverted. I had done things that I would be ashamed to tell anyone, things that I believed were unforgivable, if there was a God.

When Dave called and began reaching out to me, I

listened, but I was very critical and not open-minded to the things that he was telling me. He told me that I needed Jesus Christ. I didn't have any idea what that meant. He told me that God could save me from my sin and I didn't understand how. He told me that God had a plan for my life and it's not dying on the streets alone with nobody. Dave began to testify to me about what God had done in his life and how God had changed him. He told me that he went to a Christian program called Teen Challenge Connecticut. This was one of the strangest things that I have ever heard because not only did I not know that there was such a thing as Christian programs, but had never even known a Christian in my entire life. The first thing that my skeptical mind said was, "This guy is trying to tell me that God died for sinners and saves them when they don't deserve it and changes their lives?" I thought if this were true it would have been good information to receive from people when I'm lying face first in the gutter from an overdose, or laid up in a hospital bed, or living out in my car, or locked up behind bars or in a psychiatric hospital. But no, Dave is the only person in the world who has obtained this information about God. It was completely illogical to me for this to be something that was true, yet never brought to my attention in my 23 years of miserable existence. At the same time, it was something that I didn't completely disregard either. His words definitely had an impact on me and I began to do some thinking, especially during four days of no sleep, high on speed with my mind racing.

A few days later I entered a psychiatric hospital because I was hearing voices and having homicidal and suicidal thoughts.

I was in the hospital for three months while doctors tried to find something that would help me. The entire time I was getting high on heroin that my friends were smuggling into the hospital. I got out of the hospital and went right back to the streets. I didn't take any medical advice and wasn't taking any of the medication that the doctors had prescribed. My mental state was as bad as it has ever been. On the morning of July 20, 2011, I found out that there was a group of people looking for me because of a drug debt. I grabbed my machete and stormed out of the drug house to find them before they found me. This girl Rebecca, who was not even a close friend, saw my mental state and was very concerned as I ran down the streets of Boston looking for a group of 20 people. She told me that I needed to go back to the psychiatric hospital and get help. I told her that no one can help me so she should just stop wasting her time. She continued to follow me down the street and was persistent and finally I got in her car because she told me that she would get me drugs. We went and got high and then she brought me to the hospital. We sat in the car outside the hospital as she tried to convince me to go in and seek help.

After two hours and feeling very angry, I walked into the hospital out of control and they strapped me down and shot me up with drugs that calmed me down. When I woke up my dad was by my side as the doctors talked about another stay in the psychiatric hospital. This was when my dad spoke up and told the doctors that I've been in and out of hospitals my entire life and he really believed that I needed something else. He told the doctors that he knew about a program that I could go to in Connecticut called Teen Challenge. The doctors were skeptical and were very adamant about me going back into long-term psychiatric treatment. The doctor looked at all of my paperwork and then asked to be excused for a moment.

When she returned she explained to us that my insurance would not cover another inpatient stay at the hospital and that she was releasing me. My dad and I got in his car and he asked me if I was ready to go to Teen Challenge. He told me again some of the things that it had done in Dave's life. I told my father that I would go and he said, "Meet me at my house at 9 AM. If you are not at my house by 9 AM, you have missed your ride and you're on your own." I went out that night to get high one more time. I didn't have much money, but I drank so much that I passed out early. I woke up at 8:30 AM and I was 30 minutes away from my dad's house. As I hurried to get out of the house before anyone could stop me, I ran into one of the other addicts that had just awakened. He looked at me in shock that I was awake and that I was headed out so early when he knew that I didn't have any money to buy drugs. He said to me, "Stokes where are you going?" The words that came out of my mouth next were just as much a shock to me as they were to him. I said, "I'm going to find God." At the time I thought it was one of the strangest things to say, but looking back I don't know if there was anything else that I could have said.

We pulled up to Teen Challenge and I was barely willing to do the program. I saw some of the guys that were walking around, and I told myself that it's going to be impossible to do fifteen days, never mind fifteen months. I saw Dave for the first time in over ten years and he continued to encourage me, he told me that he believed in me, and knew that I could do this and needed to do this. The last thing that my dad said to me was that he would finally be able to sleep at night knowing that I am in a safe place. He said that every siren that he heard at night would wake him up, and he awaited the call from the authorities minutes later telling him that I died. I knew at this moment that the only hope that I had was that there was a God. Only God could save me from what I had become. If I knew how to fix this, I would have done it a long time ago.

Most of the guys in the program were not white and I

wanted very little to do with any of them. I avoided everyone for my first few days. My first week, I barely slept at all and was so uncomfortable. My skin was crawling without the drugs and I couldn't consume any solid food with out vomiting. It was like a nightmare that I just wanted to wake up from. During this time, an African American man named Bo began to reach out to me whenever he saw me. I was miserable, so most guys stayed away from me, but Bo showed an interest in my life even when it was obvious that I didn't want to be bothered. He would ask me questions about my life and about God. I would say things like, "What would God possibly want from me? There's nothing good about me and I have absolutely nothing to offer God." Then Bo began to explain God in the same way that Dave had been explaining Him to me. So my skeptical mind said, "So now there's two men in the world who know who God is?" Bo told me that I was in such a great position in my life right now when it came to God. I thought that he was insane. I questioned how my life had anything to do with a God who I was told was holy.

One day when he was talking to me, some painful memories came up and I broke down. Bo said, "Stevie there's only one question I have to ask you and when you answer this question I hope you understand how blessed you are." So I told him to ask me the question. He said, "Stevie are you lost?" With my hands over my face, crying and thinking about my life I said, "Of course I'm lost!" The next thing Bo said changed my life because it showed me who God really was. He said, "Well that's good, because God only saves lost people." Then he handed me a Bible and said, "If you don't believe me then take a look for yourself."

What Bo said set me on a mission to see if there was any validity to what he was saying. I've always been a logical person and have always understood that if there was a God then He couldn't be defined by man. I knew that if God existed, then He defined us and it didn't matter what anyone believed about Him, it wouldn't change who He was. If we could define Him then he wouldn't be God. I've always understood and believed that simple concept. I hoped with everything inside of me that this was who God was because this was the only hope that I had. I took the Bible and for the first time in my life I opened it and I had no idea where to begin reading. I just opened it and read the first verse that I saw and it was Matthew 7:13 which said, "Enter through the narrow gate. For wide is the gate and broad is the way that leads to destruction, and many enter through it. But small is the gate and narrow the way, that leads to life; and only a few find it." This seemed strange to me that the thing that I struggled with the most is that this God of the Bible seemed to be this big secret that was being kept from me and the first verse that I read explains my skepticism away in seconds.

I began to feel better physically and I spent hours down in the Learning Center reading the Bible. At the same time, I was still having outbursts of anger and I still couldn't control myself.

> My anxiety and mental condition started to impact me again and I told myself that I was no good and I had no hope.

This was a common feeling for me and usually I would have no convictions, I would run away. I never cared about hurting people or the consequences that would come from my actions. If I wanted to do something, there was no hesitation and I would act immediately. However, something was different this time. I didn't understand what was going on, but for the first time in my life I felt the weight of this decision. I knew that leaving Teen Challenge would have drastic consequences. I questioned why I would even care about consequences when I never had before. I knew that this moment in my life was much more than walking away from a program: this was a decision to walk away from Jesus Christ. This was a decision to choose death rather than life and I was ready to choose death.

My plan was to pack my bags without telling anyone. I had already set aside a few bags of cans that I could cash in. I planned to go to the projects and rob someone for some heroin and then catch a train to Boston. I was in a hurry and was happy when I got past everyone on my way to my room to pack my bag. I opened my door to my room and stopped right in front of a mirror that was on my wall. I stared at myself in the mirror, hating what I was and what I was about to do. It was an old familiar feeling, but this time I knew that God was pleading with me to surrender my life to Him. I believe that night I saw myself for what I really was. I was no longer the scared little boy who didn't know who God was; I was the monster who was ready to walk away from the God who died for me on the cross. I fell to my knees in my room and I felt the shame of everything that I have ever done and everyone that I have ever hurt. It was an experience that I never had in my life and I did the only thing that I knew to do. I got up without my bags and began to walk down the street towards a church that we attended for Friday night chapel. I was a few hours early, but I knew that the doors were usually unlocked.

I went in alone and as I walked in, I felt a peace that I had never felt before. I knew what I needed to do and that was exactly what I did. I knelt down in the front of the altar right below the cross and I said, "God I don't know how to live. Forgive me and take my life and do with it whatever you please. God I accept Jesus Christ and believe that You gave Your life for me." On August 5, 2011 Jesus Christ saved me and changed my life forever. As I walked out of that church, I felt such a hope for the first time in my life and I couldn't even explain to people what had happened to me. God delivered me from drugs and alcohol that night and I walked down the streets of New Haven, back to the center feeling like a new person.

> I remembered the words that I had said as I walked out of that crack house, "I'm going to find God."

I thought about that statement and then what Bo had told me and I said to myself, "Find God? God was never lost. God was finding me."

I began to stay up at night and read my Bible until my eyes hurt, just praying and studying. At this point in my life, I literally had nothing except for God and yet I never felt so satisfied. God was beginning to work on my heart and He took all of the hatred, prejudice, and unforgiveness from me and I began to see the entire world differently. My family began to visit me and they saw what God had done in my life and slowly I began to gain their trust back. I was shocked when my father allowed me to come to his house on my pass and trusted me to stay the night. I knew that I was changed, but I also knew that so much damage had been done and that it would take time to prove myself. I knew that I needed to be patient and not force anything, but just let God be God. I was so tired of deceiving, lying, and stealing that I gave up defending myself and my behavior and waited on the Lord to vindicate me. I knew that it was a difficult process of restoration, but that He was able.

God gave me a relationship with my family that I have never had before. He allowed me to forgive my mother and our relationship became completely changed. My cousin Derrick would come to visit me and I began to minister to him. He gave his life to Christ and now serves as a deacon at his church in Boston. God carried me through some difficult times in Teen Challenge.

I graduated and knew that God wanted me to serve Him in the ministry. He had done so much in my life and I knew that He wanted to use my life to impact other people. During my apprenticeship, I was the night supervisor and I was so privileged to be able to serve the Lord in Teen Challenge. I was shocked that I was actually getting a paycheck for being in ministry and serving the Lord. I finished my apprenticeship and in 2014, I was hired and soon after I became the Program Supervisor for Teen Challenge Connecticut. When I first started in this position, I felt so unqualified and unequipped, but like everything else I knew that with God all things were possible.

When I go back to Boston to see my family and friends, I run into people that I know every time. Most of them say, "Is that Steve Stokes? I thought that you were dead." I think to myself, "I was dead, but now I'm alive. I was lost, but now I'm found." They see my life today and can't believe that I am the same person who was the crazy drug addict they knew. I give all the glory to God and make sure that they know that I'm not ashamed of God. I am no longer on any medication and have not been since 2011. My mind is fully functioning and sane. I am still the Program Supervisor at Teen Challenge Connecticut and I really believe that working at Teen Challenge is the greatest job in the world! I am so grateful to the Lord for this ministry and the wonderful people that He has put in my life. If you told me during my intake in 2011 that I would be the Program Supervisor one day, I would have laughed. But I didn't know then, that God uses the foolish things of the world.

On May 22, 2018 I proposed to the love of my life and we are currently planning our wedding. I'm overwhelmed when I know that I was never alone and even in my darkest times on the streets crying and hoping for the pain to end, God was there. Many nights I still lay awake and cry, but now these are tears of joy as I think of what God has done for me. I am a changed life and He can change your life as well.

Chapter 5
God's Grace

Rachel Dieckhoff DiPippo

My entire life can be summed up in two powerful words – God's grace. I began my Teen Challenge journey December 26th, 1997 at the age of 19 after committing a felony. I was given the choice of prison or a program with no charges being pressed if I chose a program. It was the single most pivotal moment of my life when I entered this discipleship program. My name is Rachel, I am 39 years old and I am married to a wonderful, godly man. We have two smart and beautiful daughters, currently ages two and three, and with a heart full of gratitude I graduated Teen Challenge in April of 2000. The story I have to share is one that starts as tumultuously as everyone else who enters the program a mess, journeys through the metamorphosis of the Teen Challenge years, and highlights the adventures of a life lived for Christ.

I want to start by saying my mother did the best she

could with what she had – which was little to no support, a husband who was diagnosed with schizophrenia, three kids aged three and under when she was 23 years old, and very little income. I grew up in an apartment complex that stood as the only one in a wealthy school district on Long Island in New York and so anyone living there attending school was referred to as "as apartment kid." The name-calling started in kindergarten and persisted daily right through high school graduation. A real confidence booster – but my mother made the right decision to do whatever she could do to keep us in a school district that ranked among the top public schools in the state of New York. I was afforded in high school the opportunity to participate in college level courses.

Growing up with a schizophrenic father made for a tough childhood. My father believed he was "Father Christmas" and gave all his possessions away to strangers, or Jesus as the Son of God, or John the Baptist and baptized himself at the local beach naked, or Satan and conversed with demons, or the Anti-Christ with impending end of time doom, or some other Biblical character like Abraham, or Pan the Greek god who molests the Nymphs (and I was the nymph). In his delusional state, throughout my childhood, my father would tell me I was Gaia, the goddess of the earth. I had to learn at a young age to not believe anything that he said because it was "crazy talk." The intensity and number of bizarre events are too numerous for this story, but there are several incidents that stand out from the rest. There was a specific time when I was playing the cello for the school concert in middle school and no family members showed.

> When I went home, it happened to be that my father tried choking one of my younger brothers.

When I asked him later why he did it, he said it was because he was Abraham and the oldest son needed to be sacrificed. Another moment was when I was in the 6th grade. My brothers and I were all on the couch while our father paced back and forth ranting while in a schizophrenic state. I felt like a hostage in the living room during this psychotic episode. My father ended up in a psychiatric facility for the next six months and that was his final night living with us. An even more pronounced life-changing moment was when I found out that this man I thought was my father was indeed not. When I was 26 years old, he agreed to take a paternity test, when I learned it was a possibility that he was not biologically related. Once the results were in, I no longer felt obligated to visit him and subject myself to a toxic, inappropriate relationship.

To summarize my life before Christ, I was raised Catholic, but did not have a deep personal relationship with God. To me He was far away and I thought perhaps He forgot about me. In addition to being raised by a man with severe mental illness, my childhood contains the memory of a neighbor playing the "tickling game" as he molested me. I am pretty sure he did this to other girls because on the way to school one day a friend reached over to me to play the "tickling game" in the same manner. I felt like I grew up faster than my peers, had more responsibilities, and had more experiences. I first tried marijuana when I was eleven years old. I did it here and there but as I became an older teen, I favored alcohol for a variety of reasons: to fit in with friends, to numb my own pains, and to escape the feelings of a low self-esteem and a growing hatred of life. I was bullied at school daily; called ugly and a variety of other names because of my weight. I first started cutting around the 8th grade, which increased later on. I turned to using laxatives and resorted to binge/purge cycles when I entered college at 17 years old.

There was a choice I made at age 17 that colored the next few years grey. It was on a Tuesday two days before I was to go to college orientation. I wanted to look good and I thought that getting an all body tan was the way to do that. I worked at Fire Island for the summer and had a free ferry ride available, so I went over and found a secluded spot on a nude beach and lay out. I did not see anyone around me. A completely naked man holding a black bag approached me. I was embarrassed to be lying there on my stomach. The man was talking and at some point made reference to being in the business of drugs and showed me that he had a gun in his bag. The outcome of this moment in time was unwanted sex and flashbacks to moments in earlier childhood that were overwhelming. It was almost like I blacked out and I cannot even tell you which direction the man went. I went back home, made sure I was tested for any STDs, and on Thursday went to college orientation. I struggled with how to handle my emotions and the events that happened. I didn't go to counseling until a year later at the college campus and because a year had passed since the incident, I felt like I had no right to speak on what really happened, so I fabricated a story about an incident that took place "the previous week." However, then I was living a lie and the real issues that did take place were never dealt with.

So this is what my life looked like: drinking alcohol to the point of black outs, smoking marijuana occasionally, engaging daily in a self-destructive eating disorder, self-mutilation via cutting my arms, all leading to the point at which I used someone's social security number to access their meal account at school (because I depleted mine during the excessive binging and purging). I never ended up using that meal account in the end, but I was found out. The detective who picked me up gave me the choice basically between prison or a program, between taking a charge for felony (for using someone else's social security number) or having a clean record, a choice between a spiritual life or death. I chose life and found it at Teen Challenge.

The first six months were the toughest because I had not lived by such rules since maybe age ten. I went into the program thinking that it was not 24/7 and that I could come and go as I wanted, and maybe even continue my school classes. A daily schedule, timed showers, devotionals, chapel services, and biblical studies – it was so new to me. But then again, doing something different was what it would take to have a changed life. I was encouraged that the staff went through the program themselves, and at the same time I needed to learn that they too were human and not God. It is sometimes easy when you are searching for approval to idolize the people in leadership and be disappointed when you realize they make mistakes too. I had to become aware of people-pleasing motives within myself and I would venture to say that in those first six months, I didn't have a whole lot of introspection.

I was too busy trying to wrestle with urges to binge and purge, cut, and keep my mouth from getting me into too much trouble.

It took me a total of three years to actually complete the program of Teen Challenge. There was a lot that Jesus needed to root out of me and He chose to not overwhelm me by doing it all at once. It is like the passage of scripture in Deuteronomy 7:22 when the Lord did not drive out all the nations at once lest the beasts of field increase too quickly and overtake the Israelites. When Jesus did His work, He did it thoroughly. I was made whole and became a person who loved life, loved myself, loved others, and loved God. In the beginning I was emotionally charged each time I addressed prior traumas and I would act out rather than grab hold of spiritual principles. At one point I believed the lie in my head that life was not worth living and that I was not going to make it into heaven so I should make the process go quicker. I obtained a bottle of Naproxen and swallowed all the pills during a July 4th celebration and overdosed.

I had no intention of living. I did not tell anyone what I had done, but I couldn't hide it, as my body had gotten really sick. My liver shut down and my kidneys were failing. I was taken to the emergency room and moved to ICU. The doctor looked at me and said, "Did you think we had extra livers in stock here? You are dying a slow death and the best we can do is give you dialysis to clean your blood to prolong your life." Before they did the dialysis, a woman associated with the program named Barbara came to visit me, told me not to even say a word, and laid hands on me to pray. When she was done she said I better thank God for the healing I just got. A second blood test was done to test the level of toxicity in my blood before dialysis. The doctor returned with the first and second tests and declared that he hoped I believed in God because the test results were as if nothing happened. Even if my liver and kidneys all of a sudden were functioning, it would have taken a certain amount of time for the toxins to leave the blood. But I had been instantly healed. This was the day that I really knew God existed and did not need me to have it all together to be loved by Him. That was God's grace.

You would think with such a dramatic healing that there would also be a radical change. Some things did change right away, but I needed to heal and be honest with myself, and God. I needed to learn what to do with my emotions in an effective manner, develop a prayer life, manage my attitude in the face of the other attitudes of women in the program who were working out their own journeys, and I needed to learn to trust in God with my unknown future. I worried if I would ever be "normal" and not end up in a mental institution, be able to hold down a job and support myself, if I would ever get a degree, have a healthy marriage, and have children. Even more troubling, would I be able to live a life for Christ long-term or would it just be within the boundaries of the program that I could follow through with that faith? I circled the chapel of the Women's Home praying and declaring promises I felt God had for me and learned to speak life into these dry bones.

At some point in the program, I had decided in an

unhealthy manner to focus on "acting good" without dealing with problems. I dove into being a great student of the Bible and tried to follow the rules. I was acing the classes and I cruised along without getting into trouble for that period of time. I equated that if I talked about my past then I would become out of control, so the answer was to not talk about past trauma. This was unhealthy because the Holy Spirit would bring to light in my memory something that caused faulty thinking or negative emotions and I would shelf it all. That all exploded on me one day when we attended a conference as guests. There was a drama and the actors were playing out a domestic violence scene. The "shelf" where I shoved unwanted memories broke.

I felt broken. I was faced with two choices – be swallowed up by painful emotions or face it head on.

I stayed in limbo on making that decision and I just couldn't speak. When I finally made the decision to take a step forward and not leave the program, spend more time seeking God to heal what only He could heal and not achieve more success through classes, and when I fixed my eyes on the cross and pushed through the pain rather than run from it through acting out, only then I was able to start that journey out of the pit of despair I felt I was in.

I can say without a doubt that for those who complete

the program in its entirety, however long it takes, the path is set before you when you don't look to the left or right. Since I graduated Teen Challenge 18 years ago, I gave back four years as a staff for the Women's Home in Rhode Island while simultaneously attending Bible College. I earned a four-year Bachelor's degree in Bible with a minor in Missions and moved on to Seminary in Ohio. There I studied Clinical Pastoral Counseling with a concentration in Divinity and earned a Master's Degree. I have since been licensed as a Mental Health Counselor, worked with families of out of control teens who were court ordered to treatment because of their drug and alcohol use or poor behavior, and also had a private practice. I was able to broaden my scope of services to provide biblically based counseling while incorporating clinical tools combined with the invitation of the Holy Spirit to bring about healing in the lives of others.

I have traveled to 15 different countries for mission trips, visiting some more than once, and have given my testimony of God's grace in all of them. The highlights are: attending a Leadership Conference in Portugal to learn about starting a new Teen Challenge Program overseas and being invited to Holland to speak into the lives of future possible Teen Challenge directors while volunteering at a day program ministering to addicts at their church. I also went to Teen Challenge in Spain to help feed them during a Christmas holiday. The most memorable mission was being invited to speak into the lives of the new staff of a just-approved Teen Challenge women's home in Pakistan.

I will spend some extra time telling the details of the story of that trip to Pakistan because it was not a destination to which I really wanted to go, yet clearly God called me to go during one of my school vacations. There was one small miracle after another. I had been praying in my dorm and praying over the countries I saw on a huge map on the wall. When I looked at Pakistan I sensed God was saying to me that I would be going there during school break. So much was going on over there that surely He was not calling me there. I pulled out a phone card and called my friend who was over there who had previously extended to me an invitation to come. Besides being surprised that she actually answered the phone because I didn't even know what time it was there, she told me she couldn't believe I was calling her at that moment because she had just found out they were approved by the government to move forward with opening the women's home. She followed that up with another invitation to come and speak encouragement to the new staff since I had been both a graduate and staff of the program, to give the perspective of both sides. She also asked if I could get a laptop to bring to them as a donation for drug awareness presentations in the schools. Without thinking about it I said yes.

Changed Lives

When God says go and you say yes, He will be sure to provide what you need. I said yes with no money, didn't even own a laptop myself, and wondered if I would even be approved for a visa. I put out on social media that if anyone had a laptop they could send with me. A woman who lived in Texas, whom I met while stuck in Ethiopia for three days after missing a connecting flight back to America, wrote to me and sent me a laptop to take all the way to Pakistan. I was approved for a visa within one week of applying – in the middle of that very week, two businessmen were beheaded in the same airport I was to fly into. I was very surprised to receive an approved visa under those circumstances. As for that plane ticket, I only had a few hundred dollars in my bank account the week before school break and still had no ticket. Someone said they were going to help fund the trip but that fell through. Yet they did connect me with a travel agent who had a great price on a ticket. The travel agent called me while I was at work in the kitchen at school. I told her that I would call her back when I got to my dorm room. I left work early to go make that phone call and as I was walking across campus a friend stopped me. She said she couldn't believe she just ran into me because she had just been praying and God told her to go right then at that moment to the bank to give me the money she had in her bank account. I went with her and we moved the money from her account to mine.

When I called the travel agent, the price of the ticket was all the money I had except one dollar to keep my bank account open!

Seriously, this one small fragment of my life is enough to say how real God is in taking care of the details of our life story. (In addition to the miraculous healing He provided of course!)

God's hand got me to Pakistan, He moved during my stay, and if I went for no other reason but for what unfolded next: When leaving the country I had 30 copies of The Cross and the Switchblade in the Urdu language. I was pulled aside in the airport by armed guards who were yelling at me because they thought I was a drug mule. I answered their questions and I kept telling myself in my head, "God didn't allow you to kill yourself, and these men cannot kill you without God's permission." When they opened my luggage and looked through the books, the guard in charge asked if I knew who he was – it turned out he was the head of the anti-narcotics force for Pakistan and said he had great respect for what I do and asked for a copy of the book so that he can refer people to the program. In that country there are signs everywhere that state the penalty for drug possession is death. The possibility that a life would be spared because Teen Challenge exists in Pakistan and because I was obedient to complete the program myself was worth all the hard years.

Changed Lives

I saw God move over and over in all my travels, education, and ministry experiences. I had prayed that the Lord would have a husband for me who was "about his Father's business" as I was. It was on a mission trip when I unexpectedly came across a gentleman that I knew was to be my husband. I was almost 33 at that point and sure of what God had for me, and didn't come across the realization of that prayer until it was the perfect time. We learned that we had over 40 of the same close friends through church and that he even made a meal that I ate while on staff at Teen Challenge and visiting his church. We both remembered the day but did not remember meeting. Then while on a double date with friends of his we found out they tried to connect us together eight years prior. Long story short, because of the obedience to allow God to do the work He needed to do, we have a healthy marriage of almost seven years and are raising our daughters in the faith and teachings of Jesus, being lead by the Holy Spirit as we parent the next generation of world changers.

I think of Teen Challenge as an emergency incubator that saved my life from myself, and prepared me for a life living out a mission for God. Today I have lived just as many years post-Teen Challenge as I did pre-Teen Challenge. God's grace took me from the destructive path I was forging and He set me on His path. My life has been filled with love, joy, and peace, and we look forward to God's continued blessings which would not have been made possible if I had not entered Teen Challenge. I was given the best possible gift that day – LIFE. The scripture I have always held onto is James 1:2-4 which states, "Consider it pure joy my brothers whenever you face trials of many kinds, because you know that the testing of your faith develops perseverance, and perseverance must finish its work so that you may be mature and complete, not lacking anything." I want you to know that what Teen Challenge and the Lord gave me can also be yours - a changed life!

Chapter 6
On The Other Side

Scott O'Neil

All my life I have been a dreamer, incessantly day dreaming about the fascinating things of the world. As young as I can remember I was one of the most gullible children in the universe. My interest was always sparked by almost everything. I fantasized about being the next best next football, basketball, or baseball player, or even martial artist. The thrill of the games captured everything inside of me, from watching Red Sox pitcher Pedro Martinez on the pitcher's mound striking out many a foe all the way to the excitement of watching the Patriot's Drew Bledsoe throw to Ben Coates in the end zone. These things always made my heart leap.

I didn't know what I wanted to be, but I wanted to be something great, something that would continue to challenge me and make me feel like a superhero. I used this ambition to fuel my life to be the best at everything, a true natural competitor. It was most exciting for me was when someone told me I couldn't do something. I would accept the challenge and take pride in proving them wrong. When I was about twelve years old, I remember being told I was too overweight and short to be successful in any sports at about 5'4" and 160 lbs. My support group wasn't very big at the time, my parents believed in me, but we weren't quite "in" with the politics of the local sports groups and I always felt like somewhat of an outcast.

Wanting to be able to play football, I took a shot at a pop warner team. The parents were ever so serious and I had never felt more of that "not fitting in" feeling in all my life. No one took me under their wing and at twelve years old I was overwhelmed playing with the fourteen-year-olds. I quit after only a few short weeks, disappointed and saddened that I couldn't play the sport I had dreamed of for so long. It didn't look that hard when I watched them on TV? Who knows, maybe I just wasn't ready, but looking back, I know that the lack of encouragement from others played a huge role. At this point in my life, I'd already had a few years of playing basketball and baseball, but football was special to me and I couldn't shake the fact that I had failed at something I wanted to be good at. My dreams were crushed.

Not long after I started working out with a good friend of mine who was serious about weightlifting. We would go to the YMCA every single day after school and spend hours there. We worked out for two hours and then we would go play basketball or something in the gym. This was a huge part of my life because this is when I started to develop physically. It also kept me out of trouble with the many temptations that came from the streets. Things really started to turn around for me physically by the time I got to the 8th grade at 14 years old I was about 5'8" and 170 lbs.

Another one of my good friends played for the junior high school football team and urged me to come out and give it a try. Timid that I would fail again, I gave it a go and instantly fell back in love with the dream of being a football player. I was stronger and bigger now and able to take the hits I couldn't take before. My pain threshold had increased tremendously and I was ready to compete again. My work ethic in the gym continued and I was able to get a starting spot on my 9th grade junior high school team and was named a captain. This gradual increase in athleticism continued to high school where

I became a captain in my senior year of the football team and received All-State recognition.

As a shot putter, I competed at the Nike Indoor Nationals and finished in the top ten and was an undefeated outdoor shot put champion winning all the way up to Regional/New England Championship.

Changed Lives

The New England Championship was held on the same day of my graduation, and having come in second at the indoor New England Championship, I was determined to win. At the time, I didn't have the best throw in the region; there was someone who threw further. His name was "Bruce," a staggering 6'7" and 280 lb man who could launch the stone like no other. He later became an offensive tackle in the NFL. The pressure was heightened because my future college coaches from Southern Connecticut State University were attending the meet. Yet, I didn't let that throw me off. I was all in at this point.

Bruce's first throw of the meet was a booming 58 feet 6 inches. No one had thrown that far all year and he knew that, taunting that he "doesn't even have to throw no more" after dropping that bomb. I came to my final three throws of my high school career and the pressure never felt so strong. I was in second place but determined not to lose, I let it all fly. My first throw was about 57 feet. The second throw was a foul and it all came down to the last throw of my high school career. I still remember approaching the circle with adrenaline rushing through my veins, headstrong to finish my dream of being the New England shot put champion. I let my final throw go. I remember watching the shot land and the crowd go completely silent as they saw the distance and knew it was going to be close.

I knew I gave it my all and that this was the furthest throw of my life. As the officials read the tape, it felt like my fate was being read in a national court case. The officials read the tape "58 feet, 6 AND A HALF inches." I won the championship by a half inch! Word boomed all around my town and the local newspaper called me as soon as I got home. This was the most satisfying athletic accomplishment of my life and was a trophy of what hard work can do. Discipline, encouragement from others, and a good support group did wonders for somebody who was told so many times he couldn't be good at anything and would always be average.

Heading to Southern Connecticut State University, I felt on top of the world and my life seemed to be falling into place. My party life at this point had been out of control, but I hadn't suffered any consequences from it and continued to party. I smoked a lot of marijuana and got black-out drunk all the time with my friends. This continued into college and I started losing control. My pride over everything I accomplished my senior year gave me the attitude of "I got this." But I was a deceived 18-year-old heading to college, prideful, arrogant, and unwilling to take advice when it came to drugs and alcohol.

Smoking marijuana was a favorite for me. I started showing up to practices high. At morning practices I would arrive hung over. I couldn't keep up with it all anymore. When I was cornered by my habits because my grades were lacking and my performance athletically was declining, I folded and dropped out. This is when things got tremendously worse in my life.

When I got home from school, I faced the reality that my life and dreams were shattered and I couldn't bear it emotionally. How did I go from a high school champion to a bum so quickly? Why did I let it progress so far and never bear down and make it right? Who knows, but for me it was much easier to drink and smoke weed all the time.

A good friend I grew up with since I was seven years old, since our dads were always close, had taken paths to different high school.

He started using OxyContin and just happened to swing by to hang out. Seeing my turmoil, he asked me if I wanted to try some.

I said "sure" and my life changed dramatically after that first line.

He and I started doing a lot more drugs and selling drugs together. We became best friends again and were making enough money selling cocaine and weed to keep our Oxycontin habits. Soon we started shooting heroin. It was a cheaper and a faster fix for the withdrawals that every addict is familiar with.

I was 19 years old; shooting heroin, cocaine, and

smoking crack on a regular basis, running through life like a fiend, ruining relationships, and decimating everything I loved. Trying to be introspective at times, I tried to "find myself" in this mess. Somehow the drug culture makes you feel a part of something. It's hard to describe, but it makes you feel important. It is an artificial feeling though, because your "drug buddies," for the most part, don't care about you. It's a selfish game; rob whomever to get whatever so that you don't have to deal with your issues or your problems.

During this time period I lost one of my best high school friends to a heroin overdose. He was 19 and a brilliant "A" student at the University of New Hampshire's school of business. Everyone loved him because his willingness to defend those who were regarded as less than others. I'll never forget the phone call from one of my friends that he had overdosed. I had just talked to him the day before. This wrecked my world.

I went even deeper and harder after drugs. At one point while with my best friend and another guy picking up drugs in Lawrence, Massachusetts, he took a shot of dope in the backseat. I looked back and saw he wasn't breathing and turning blue. With fear crippling my entire being that I was going to lose another best friend I jumped out of the passenger's seat and ran to the back and threw him on to the side of the road. I began to give him CPR rapidly and slap him across the face to get his nerves going again. To the glory of God and only by His grace did my best friend come back to life. But still, this didn't change us, and it wasn't enough of a wakeup call to seek help.

Addiction had stripped me of everything. My soul had never been in such poverty, defeat, and complete horror that this might be my life forever. I remember being arrested for breaking into cars not long after these events and looking in the mirror and not recognizing the lifeless creature I had become: pupils swollen from withdrawal and a whopping 180 lbs. at 6'3". I didn't want to do this anymore. I tried the methadone clinic and that didn't work. I couldn't afford a rehab program because I didn't have insurance, and there was no way my family could pay for it because both of my parents were on disability.

Days were long and painful; all the healthy relationships in my life were destroyed. I felt trapped and everything felt so dark with no hope. Empty and morally bereft, any hint of character I had was gone. I could have done anything to anybody for anything at this point. It was like there was a monster living inside of me.

Then one day I asked the father of my best friend that I had performed CPR on where he had gone, since I hadn't heard from him in a while. His dad told me that he went to a 15-month program called Teen Challenge. He recommended it because he said they might be able to take me in even though I didn't have money to go.

My mom was optimistic about it and knew I needed it. My family swayed me to try it. I had pending charges over my head after breaking into cars and I was facing either jail time or rehab. Feeling pressured to make a decision I decided to go to Teen Challenge. The admissions coordinator told me everything I needed to hear. He sounded so confident, sharing stories of people who had made it successfully, including himself. He also told me it would be the hardest thing I would ever do yet assured me support would be there. I believed him.

On February 21st, 2011 on President's Day, I came through the doors of Teen Challenge New Hampshire still kind of high from some weed that I had smoked and Suboxone that I had taken before going.

But for the first time ever I felt peace and a Presence that I had never felt before in my life.

A soft whisper came to my soul and spirit that said, "You don't ever have to go back to that lifestyle again. This can be over for you." I now know it to have been the voice of God bringing comfort to my affliction. I was greeted by my best friend and we enjoyed our time through Teen Challenge together. He mentored me through the program, taught me about scripture and led me into a great relationship with the Lord. I couldn't believe the change I saw in him, he was totally different. God was real to me because Jesus had changed my best friend's life dramatically. If He could do it for him, then I knew that God could do it for me.

As we traveled to churches across New Hampshire and Massachusetts, my best friend and I had the honor of sharing our testimonies together about how God had saved us both. About how I was able to save his life while he was overdosing and then how God used his life to save me for eternity. When I talk to people to this day, I always mention this significant part of our life because of how unique it is.

We also had the opportunity to travel to many high schools to share our story about how drugs ruined our lives. We couldn't share about God, but we were able to inform students about the decisions they can make in life. How one day you could be an 18-year-old local athlete with potential college scholarships and the next day be a 19-year-old crack cocaine and heroin addict. I don't think there was a class that didn't have a look of shock and awe when we told them about the overdosing in Lawrence, Massachusetts and how any day could be the last for any of their friends that choose to use opiates.

Teen Challenge is a place of refuge for the suffering addicts in the world. They gave me an opportunity when I didn't have any. It was God's avenue to literally save my life. I had never heard the good news about Jesus before Teen Challenge and never really thought about God, but that all changed thanks to the ministry of Teen Challenge.

My time there wasn't easy, it was very difficult. I was forced to face my personal issues, become better with people, and make the right choices not to get involved with nonsense when staff wasn't around. We worked hard, were given discipline for not following the structure or having a bad attitude, all of which God used to turn me into who I am today. Learning about Jesus was the most important part of it all, but being there, you learn from others. You learn about proper hygiene, adulthood, leadership, about mistakes that other guys made as parents. I saw the pain of the older guys who had lived their entire lives as addicts and now wish they had gotten help even ten years earlier. But, glory to God that He can use anyone at any age to do anything for His purpose. And I certainly didn't take that for granted.

Convinced that I wanted to give back and minister to hurting people who were like me, I stayed on with Teen Challenge for another five or so years to pay forward the service that others had given me. In that time, I saw so many lives changed, families restored, and God's glory in the work of people. God led me to get my ministerial credentials with the Assemblies of God, and I became a youth pastor at a church from my hometown of Nashua, New Hampshire. My best friend was also a youth pastor at a different church in Nashua. God has done such wonderful things in my life and I'm forever grateful. I am a changed life!

God has blessed me with a wonderful wife, Christina. We got married in March of 2015 and I have been so grateful to have such a person by my side.

> I never thought I would be married, have a family, or make it out of addiction.

The most famous parts of scripture are when you don't think anything is possible, there is always "But God." My faith was formed in affliction. When darkness was increasing that only a Marvelous Light would be able to overcome it, He did.

As I write this chapter, I am in my apartment in Louisiana. I work a secular job and attend an amazing church. Christina and I patiently await the call of God for our next chapter. I want to close my story with a letter to an addict that I wrote as a blog post for Teen Challenge.

Dear Friend,

The first thing I want to tell you is that you can have a brighter future. Yesterday doesn't have to define you, and I understand that there is a lot of uncertainty about today. I have been where you are with this addiction. Right now you are probably thinking that you need money to get the next

high and where is that going to come from? Is someone after me, or is someone going to rob me? Do I still have any "real" friends or are we just friends because we use drugs together? Am I going to die today? Will my life end as an addict and never accomplish anything in my life? What is my purpose? I have felt your loneliness and the feeling of abandonment, the emptiness that seems to rule your life. Drugs seem to kill all the pain and put you back into your groove, I have been there.

I get the feeling of not wanting to do this anymore but you don't know where to turn. Friends have stopped supporting you; parents don't want anything to do with you, and the only ones that seem to be pursuing you are drug friends and the police department. I have shared in your tears and the deep depression after the drugs are gone, and reality sets in, where the feeling of sobriety becomes unbearable.

But my plea to you friend is despite what you might be thinking, this can come to an end. I write you having come through the other side of addiction. It was the hardest thing I have ever done, but it couldn't have been any more rewarding. On the other side of addiction there is a bright future waiting for you, a person you don't even know within yourself. You make it through this and you will be stronger then you ever could imagine. People will see your determination and perseverance from something that seems to have no cure. Freedom can be yours, trust me I am experiencing it myself!

Changed Lives

Know there is hope for tomorrow. If you choose the path that I did and seek a relationship with Jesus Christ, I know that He will not let you down, even if you feel He has let you down in the past. Even if you never had believed in God, as I did an atheist, God wants to save you from many things, but your addiction is a high priority to Him. Jesus once said, "The Spirit of the Lord is on me, because he has anointed me to proclaim good news to the poor. He has sent me to proclaim freedom for the prisoners and recovery of sight for the blind, to set the oppressed free." (Luke 4:18). As I write this letter I am approaching five years of sobriety myself and have a brighter future then I ever could have imagined. Today I am a youth pastor at my church, and work as an Administrator at Teen Challenge, the organization that Jesus used to save and give me a new life.

Even if you do not choose my route, as much as I would encourage you to, I sincerely hope that you would seek help. That you would stop running from the people you love and start to take the steps towards sobriety. Be real with yourself as you contemplate this, don't think you can do it alone, and don't fool yourself or anyone else by saying things such as "I will start tomorrow" or "Let me get high one more time and think about this," start today, start NOW.

With much love from your friend on the other side,
Scott O'Neil

Chapter 7
I Lost Everything

Derek Correa

I grew up in Lawrence, Massachusetts. It was and is a pretty rough place, and is a major hub for narcotic trafficking and distribution in New England.

My family felt the effect of living in a city so affected by drug use. My father tried heroin when he was eleven years old. My mother had an alcoholic father and was no less prone to experimenting with drugs and alcohol in her teens. My parents met at the tender age of fourteen and started dating soon after. Because both of them came from families in which addiction was commonplace, it was not surprising that they found themselves in their own cycle of drug and alcohol abuse.

In a sense, my sister and I were born into a lifestyle of dysfunction because of our parent's choices. My father was a full blown heroin addict by the time my sister was born. My sister, nine years older than me, saw much more of the effects of my father's role in our household. My father was extremely abusive to my mother for years. By the time she was pregnant with me at age 27, she realized that she needed to make a break from the chaos of her marriage. She knew that if she didn't, she would be bringing her next child into a situation where things would likely only get worse.

I never met my biological father. She left him before I was born. Unfortunately, as necessary as that was, it did not solve all my mother's problems. All she had known until that point was dysfunction. All she had ever seen was unhealthy relationships, so it wasn't too long before she gravitated towards another man who had a similar interest in "having a good time."

Michael was the only father figure I knew and he was a lot nicer guy than my real father. He was always good to us. He practiced what I call "the weekend warrior" type of lifestyle. He and my mom were responsible hardworking people Monday – Friday, but come Friday night the party was on. I'm convinced that by observing this for years, I assumed that this was the way of life as an adult. You go to work on time, you pay your bills on time, you put food on the table every week, and as long as you've lived up to those ideals, you were free to do as you please come the weekend. To be honest it made perfect sense to me.

I can remember even as a kid practicing the same type

of routine. Go to school every day, do my homework, get good grades, do my chores and then whatever time was left over was mine to do what I wanted. The problem with that lifestyle is that I began to cultivate a habit of rewarding myself for whatever I did that seemed praiseworthy or good in my own eyes. By the time I got to high school that habit would produce self-destructive pattern.

When I was twelve years old my stepfather, Michael, was killed in a car accident. The year before, my mother's father committed suicide. Dealing with two major tragedies in our family in such a short span of time was more than my mother could handle. Instead of waiting for the weekend to get the party started, it became common to see her drinking any day of the week to try and numb the incredible feeling of loss and emptiness in our home.

Despite the addiction and chaos, my mother and I were always very close, but I needed a father figure and there was no one to fill that role, so I began to pull away from home life.

I chose to be out with friends rather than be at home where my mother was drowning her sorrows in a bottle.

By the time I got to high school I developed a taste for marijuana and alcohol. It seemed the most effective way for me to escape the whirlwind of emotion and confusion I was experiencing at home. I could smoke a little weed or drink a few beers and it was like "everything's all good". I fell in love with any substance that would do the trick. It was so instant! It was such a relief from what seemed like the weight of the world on my shoulders. Although some of the awful feelings may have gone away for a time, my problems were still there waiting for me when the drugs wore off.

When I was 16 years old, I had an encounter with God that I never forgot. It happened after running from the issues at home and making an entirely new life for myself with a bunch of new friends on the other side of town.

This group of friends was all I knew for about four years, but drugs, alcohol, and romantic relationships between people in our group ran their course. One day, out of nowhere, it was all over. That group of friends just broke up. Because it was all I knew, I was devastated. Suddenly I felt so alone, and the weight of all that I had been distracting myself from for those four years seemed to fall on me that one night.

As I walked home feeling so overwhelmed that I couldn't even face talking to my mother, I broke down sobbing outside. All the emotion and pain and confusion that I had been stuffing down since my stepfather died came out. While on my knees sobbing I cried out to God in the midst of all the pain. That was the first time I ever sensed the presence of God in my life. I had a peace in me that I had never known before. From that moment on I believed in God. He had made

Himself real to me. But it would be years before I would begin to seek Him again.

Through high school I practiced the weekend warrior routine. I'd work hard at my schoolwork maintaining "honor roll" status each year, and every weekend was a party. Every bit of free time I had I was high and/or drunk. I graduated from vocational high school with honors as an electrician apprentice. I loved my trade. Once again I had a reason to feel good about accomplishing something. I got affirmation from my boss and the other guys at work who thought I was a hard worker and a good apprentice. So naturally I gravitated towards the culture of the trade. I saw that even those guys thought it was perfectly normal to bust your butt all week and then reward yourself with alcohol or whatever your vice was on the weekends.

When I was 19 I tried cocaine for the first time at a party at the house I was living in with three other friends.

From that moment I was hooked on coke. It was the beginning of a long relationship with my drug of choice.

Every weekend for the next six years would include spending most, if not all, of my hard-earned money on cocaine.

Cocaine use eventually took me to the place where I would hit rock bottom. When I was 25 and living in Lynn, Massachusetts, far from any family and friends, I began to feel isolated. I was now using by myself, cooped up in my room for days at a time. I was a full-blown functioning addict. Using drugs was no longer fun for me. And honestly it didn't even feel good anymore. It was now something I had developed such a habit of doing that I felt obligated to do it every weekend. I didn't know what life looked like without drugs, so I could never get the courage to try something different. The reality was, I was miserable. I was so empty; it felt like I was just a shell of a man. Just a body, hollow on the inside. I no longer had a sense of purpose in my life. The drugs I loved for so long had taken the place of any meaningful relationships that I had with people.

I was enslaved to a lifestyle that left me the most miserable person I knew. One Sunday morning, strung out from two days without sleep or food and completely broke, I crawled off my bed and onto the floor and on my knees. I begged God to save me. I begged Him in no uncertain terms to help me! I could not go another minute in the life I was living. And you know what? God saved me! He answered my cry for help! In that moment He filled me with His Holy Spirit. I had never felt so alive. At that moment I knew He had heard me. I knew He had answered my prayer for help. All that time I had spent chasing a feeling from a drug, all the energy I spent looking for a high, I realized in those next few moments that all along it was Him I needed. It was His Holy Spirit who was the only one who could ever fill me the only one who could ever satisfy my soul.

God led me to read the Bible and I started to believe that the Bible was not just a book, but it really was God's word. I started seeing for myself that God could never have helped me, He never could have forgiven me for all I had done, if the Lord Jesus Christ had not paid for my sins. God was showing me in His word how Christ was the Son of God in the flesh! I remember being blown away at the thought that God's own Son became a man like me and was actually crucified on a cross in order to pay the penalty for my sins, so God could extend forgiveness. Life would never be the same.

I wish I could say that from that moment on I made no further bad choices in life and that everything fell into place for me. But the reality is that was not the case. As much as I was a changed man, I still had a lot of maturing to do. I was walking with God faithfully for about two years when I bought my first home. I was finally handling my money in a productive way. I had been a licensed electrician for about five years by then. As good as all that was, there were still some real compromises in my life. God had delivered me from a cocaine addiction seemingly instantly, but I was still smoking marijuana. I also had a long history of watching pornography. These habits would eventually contribute to me backsliding from my relationship with God.

Changed Lives

The day I moved into my new home I ran into a person I had been friends with when I was a teenager. After catching up on old times for a while and with all the feelings of nostalgia, we had a few beers and smoked some weed.

Before I knew it, I was doing a line of cocaine. That's all it took to get the snowball moving down the hill again.

I was so ashamed of myself and the guilt was weighing on my heart because I knew what I was heading for. In no time I was living like a functioning addict again. But this time around was very different from before. All those years before I didn't have God's Holy Spirit in me. In times past I had no real relationship with God. In times past there was no heaviness in my heart when I sinned against God. Now all that was different. Every day that I was running from God I could feel it. He literally would not allow me to enjoy getting high. I could no longer enjoy the sin I once loved, and I realized that I now loved the God I once rebelled against. Even with all that being true, because of the nature of addiction, I had to lose everything in order for me to surrender my life to Him again and that's exactly what happened.

I lost my job, then my house, and then my truck. I was living in a tent by the Merrimack River in Lowell, Massachusetts. My mother and the rest of my family was crushed. It was at that time I first heard of Teen Challenge.

My mother was now a born again Christian. She had given her life to Christ a few years before and was walking faithfully with God. He did an amazing work in my mother's life! One day Teen Challenge had come to her church to do a presentation and she heard the testimonies of the men who had gone through the program. She told me she just knew that was the place for me. It took me about a year from the first time she told me about it to agree to go. To be honest I was terrified. A fifteen-month program with sixty other people from all walks of life living in one place! Coming from living in a tent for a year out in the woods, it was not the easiest transition for me. I felt socially awkward, to say the least.

Looking back now, Teen Challenge in Brockton was the best thing I've ever done, outside of getting married. It was also the most challenging thing I've ever experienced, outside of being married. It was exactly what I needed. And I'm convinced that a program like Teen Challenge is the very thing that many addicts need. Because although I was a Christian and God had done an amazing work in my life, I was still very immature in many ways. That's what being an addict from youth does to a person. Your growth is stunted in so many ways. I had developed bad habits as an addict that followed me even into sobriety. God used the Bible, the intense structure, the constant accountability, and the relationships I developed at Teen Challenge to bring about fundamental changes in my character as a man. I am far from perfect today, but I can honestly say I am a changed man.

It's easy to look back at my time at Teen Challenge in summary fashion, looking at all the highlights. But going through real challenge and real growth is very uncomfortable at times. For example, the first few weeks at Teen Challenge were like an emotional roller coaster for me. I was relieved to not be living outside in a tent somewhere, but that sort of relief did not eliminate the physiological anxiety putting chemicals into your body every day for years is bound to cause once you decide to stop using. There were times when I felt like I was on top of the world, but by the next day I felt like I could vomit from feeling so anxious and overwhelmed by the new environment.

There were a few things that helped me to get through these times. First of all, God's Holy Spirit gave me peace and strength at the very times I needed it most. Those moments when I needed God the most He continued to make Himself real to me in the same way He did when I first cried out to Him.

As much as I needed God's help, I also needed to believe that people cared about me. Now I'd be lying if I made it seem like every person at the program was a wonderful person and were just dying to help me at every turn. That's simply not the case. But what is true is that there were a few very sincere people who encouraged me along the way. I was able to observe certain guys over time and learn from them. I have found that often times that's all I really needed for help: a few sincere people who are committed to growing in Christ. I learned from those few people and drew from their knowledge and experience, and it helped me get on the right path. God knew I needed that and it was enough to help me when I needed it the most.

I saw a few guys that set the example of servanthood. That's exactly what stood out to me. It stood out to me because when I read about Jesus Christ, I continually saw His example of servanthood. He was the very Son of God and yet He was the servant of servants. He left His throne in heaven and came to serve sinful men like me. So when I saw guys who were once addicts like I was, once self-serving, self-centered people like I had been, who were now deliberately choosing to practice a lifestyle of helping others, it affected me greatly. I wanted to be that type of guy.

> I saw guys who lived daily with a sense of purpose and a joy that no addict I'd ever known had.

God began to create a passion in me to make my life about others, not about me. This was a huge turning point in my life. I've never felt more alive than I did when I began to serve God and not myself. I started to see God use me to encourage other guys who were struggling. I started to experience the power of God's Holy Spirit when I'd talk to guys about what God was teaching me in the Bible. It seemed like there was just one opportunity after another to help someone else.

Teen Challenge gives people the opportunity to get up and go to work on a daily basis. This was so important for me. I had been working since I was sixteen years old. I got into the electrical trade when I was a sophomore in high school and had found such a sense of purpose in working with my hands. I know now that a man's work is one of God's many gifts. He gives us talents and abilities that can be used in so many positive ways. But for about two years before going to Teen Challenge I wasn't working. Being so wrapped up in drugs I couldn't function like a normal person anymore. So when I got the opportunity to do electrical work in the program, it was like a reunion for me to do the type of work I loved so much. Only this time I would not be getting paid for it, at least not for a while. But that was perfectly fine with me because I knew that I wasn't there to profit financially. I knew that I didn't even have the ability to handle money responsibly. I could now use my skills in a setting I hadn't experienced before. I was part of the maintenance/construction ministry. We did everything from electrical to plumbing and HVAC to carpentry and landscaping. Some guys got a chance to work at a trade they never would have been able to outside of Teen Challenge.

Eventually, because of the way God was working on my character, I became a leader in my ministry. I was now responsible for other guys in the program. That really helped me to mature, because there's something about being responsible for someone else's well-being that motivates you to rise to the occasion. Looking back, I can see how God was using that leadership position to prepare me for my own family and for the role I would eventually play in my local church.

Today I am married to my first and only wife Claudia. We're raising two kids (and God willing, many more). I am praying that God will break the cycle of addiction in my family and lead them to Christ at a young age. God has given me the grace to start my own electrical business which I began immediately after I left Teen Challenge. I have to say that I literally owe my life to the Lord Jesus Christ for all He has done for and in me, because I know that through my ups and downs and everything in between, He is sustaining me. I'm realizing the longer I walk with God, it's grace, upon grace, upon grace. He never changes. "For by the grace of God I am what I am, and His grace to me was not without effect." (1 Corinthians 15:10). And it is that grace that changed my life!

Chapter 8
Changed Lives

Neal & Kristy Rapoza

Kristy's Story

It's almost as if I was destined for failure before I was even born. When my mother was pregnant with me, my father got sentenced to ten years in prison, so growing up I just thought it was normal to go visit your daddy behind those prison walls. Although my mother never had a drug or alcohol problem, she had a lot of anger. I remember getting hit on a regular basis. Whipped by belts, pulling out chunks of my hair, you name it. That did something to me. It turned me into a violent person, almost as if I took on the same characteristics as my mother. My grandfather basically raised me from the time I was born. He was like my angel sent from heaven. He loved me unconditionally and would do absolutely anything in the world for me. I took him for granted most of my life, unfortunately, and I never really saw him as a good thing that

I had.

I started getting in fistfights at school and I soon took on the role as the "tough girl" which I seemed to love. For some sick reason I enjoyed hurting other people. I began living a criminal lifestyle earlier than my teenage years which landed me in countless juvenile lock up facilities. My mother always told me that I wouldn't graduate high school or make anything of myself, but one thing that I always had inside of me was determination. When those words were spoken over me, it lit a fire inside of me to prove her wrong and everybody else that ever doubted me.

> The day before my 17th birthday I was released from a maximum security juvenile lock up and for the first time in my life I was considered homeless.

Living in survival mode, I somehow managed to get a high school diploma and actually enrolled myself into college. Throughout this whole time I casually drank and did drugs but it was nothing that was out of my control. I had a couple of arrests here and there for minor things, but nothing that would have landed me in prison.

In 2008, after my grandfather died, I stopped caring about life. I tried heroin for the first time and I instantly loved the way it made me feel. Slowly, I developed a habit and started selling drugs just to be able to afford it. I started my own escort business and I made more money than I even knew what to do with. I didn't care that I degraded myself, I didn't care that I put myself in the most dangerous situations possible. In fact, I didn't actually care if I lived or died. I started doing "speedballs" mixing crack and heroin together which brought my drug habit to an all-time high, and I quickly started to lose everything.

Before I knew it I lost my apartment and found myself sleeping in abandoned apartment buildings, walking the streets during the day to support my habit. Deep down inside I knew it was only a matter of time before I ended up in prison or dead. I was sleeping in the basement of a crack house with my friend, who was six months pregnant at the time, when a man showed up with a rosary necklace and told me that he was praying for me. I brought it inside to show my friend who happened to be a backslidden Christian. Right there in the dirty, filthy, disgusting basement we talked about Jesus for hours. I got down on my knees covered in dirt and asked Him into my heart. Obviously I didn't know how to be a Christian because I was a full-blown drug addict, but I never questioned if it was true or not, I just believed. Less than a week later I was arrested on five counts of narcotics sales. I now know that was God's hand ripping me out of that life. I remember sitting in the back of the police car and just thinking to myself, "It's finally over. I never have to go back to my old life again. This is my chance." I started going to church in jail and reading my Bible and a friend told me about a wonderful program called Teen Challenge. It was the only program that accepted me when I had nothing, not even health insurance.

I entered the program in March 2011 and the moment I walked into the doors of the home I instantly felt the love of God. With tears of joy streaming down my face, I was overcome with gratitude and joy knowing that I was right where God wanted me to be. I started learning about the Bible and God started to renew my mind. My old thought patterns seemed to change rather quickly as the things of this world became less appealing, and even the way that I spoke changed. I began to respect and love myself. When I first came into the program I had absolutely no self-worth and every day I would look in the mirror and say, "You're beautiful." It took me ten months to actually believe those words.

God slowly drew the anger out of me and helped me live peacefully among other people. He began to restore the broken relationship I had with my mother and after seeing the evidence of my changed life, she started to believe. He also restored my relationship with my father and not only used me as an example, but an encouragement to him while he still battles his addictions.

> I had a lot of rage inside me before I knew Christ, but God radically took that from me and filled my empty heart with so much grace and love.

I felt like my life had purpose for the first time ever.

Through the ministry of Teen Challenge Rhode Island I began to have desires that I could never picture for myself like traveling, missionary work, and being a wife and mother someday. I knew my heavenly Father loved me and that His plan for my life was far greater than I could ever imagine. I had a deep desire to help women out on the streets and would find myself looking out the window and praying for the ones I saw. I knew I wanted to work with the homeless and that God had allowed me to go through that time in my life so that I can spread hope to people out there who can't see a future for themselves.

After completing the Teen Challenge program, I went on to be the house manager of a Christian transitional home where I got to help the lives of many women walking through the doors. I started serving with a homeless ministry and watched the desires that God placed in my heart come to life. I also began doing my own street ministry, and even got to rescue some hurting women off the streets.

Neal's Story

I grew up the youngest child in a middle class family.

I have two great, loving parents who always went above and beyond to provide for my older sister and me. Even though I had a great childhood, something always felt off. From a young age I was uncomfortable in my own skin. I was always full of anxiety and struggled with depression. I felt less than everyone else for some reason.

When I was in middle school I started experimenting with smoking marijuana and drinking alcohol. When I was either high or drunk the uncomfortable feeling that consumed my life seemed to disappear. Throughout high school, I continued to chase that high that calmed my nerves with relatively no consequences. I was an "ok" student, a standout athlete in wrestling and baseball, and always the "life of the party." Around my junior year I was introduced to OxyContin and it was like love at first sight.

A weekend binge turned into a daily routine in only a few weeks. By the time I started college at University of Massachusetts in Dartmouth, I was a full-blown addict. Those little pills started dictating every aspect of my life. I needed them just to function and live my life. The cost of getting high got to a point where I was spending upwards of $300 a day just so I wouldn't be sick. I started stealing money from my job, friends, and family. My addiction came to a point where I could no longer hide it from anyone. I was forced to drop out of college and started what seemed to be an endless cycle of programs, rehabs, and institutions. I moved from my home in Massachusetts to California, to Florida, to New Jersey, to Boston, back home, then to Connecticut.

Early on in my seemingly endless list of places I lived, while in Delray Beach, Florida, a friend introduced me to heroin and that was when my addiction went to a new low. The things I did to get the drugs became more and more desperate. I would break into houses and cars and steal from any job I had. I would do whatever I had to do to not be sick and to get high. When my life would get to complete chaos, I would move to a different part of the country, enter another rehab program, get out, and be well on my way to another relapse and more terrible decisions. While living in a Boston sober house I relapsed, and while driving my girlfriend's car. I overdosed behind the wheel as I pulled out onto a busy street. The police found me with the car in drive and my foot on the brake. I was barely brought back to life by the paramedics, but that was still not enough to make me stop using.

From there, I talked my mom into allowing me to live back at her house. That was short-lived and ultimately I entered another rehab facility in Connecticut. After only a week in the program, my insurance denied the claim because I had been in so many rehabs. I ended up leaving the program and lived with a friend I had met there, and her family. I got a job and actually had a somewhat normal three or four months before my life was out of control. I started drinking and using heroin again. My addiction got to a point where I was homeless living in the streets of New Haven, Connecticut. I was on the verge of going to prison because of a few different arrests and I was completely hopeless.

> At that point in my life I actually accepted the fact that I was going to die an addict.

It gave me some sort of demented peace because I felt like I didn't have to fight it anymore. Every time I shot up, I did so with the hope that I wouldn't wake up.

My sister Lauren and brother-in-law Justin were driving up from their home in Maryland for a friend's wedding and decided to try and find me to either "talk some sense into me, or say their final goodbyes." The exact details of the day are still really foggy, but I remember talking to my sister in the morning and telling them approximately where I was on Route 1 because I had gotten kicked out of the truck stop I was sleeping at. That entire day I spent walking up Route 1 in Connecticut, with nowhere to go, nobody to talk to, no money, food, and finally out of drugs. I vividly remember asking a God I didn't believe in to end my life. I debated walking out into oncoming traffic for the better part of an day, but for some reason I couldn't bring myself to do it.

It was the first week of July and it was really hot outside.

I ended up passing out on the side of the road. When I opened my eyes, my sister and brother-in-law were sitting beside me. My sister had her head on my shoulder and she was crying. That's an image I will never ever forget. A long story short, I ended up in their truck on my way back home so I could turn myself into my probation officer in Boston on Monday morning. Over that weekend, my Dad talked me into going to Teen Challenge in Brockton, Massachusetts. Honestly, I really didn't want to go to another program, especially a 15-month Christian program. But I pretty much had no other options and figured my probation officer would be less likely to lock me up if I was getting treatment. Through God's grace, when I turned myself in, the judge gave me yet another chance even though my probation officer wanted to lock me up.

On July 11, 2012 I walked through the doors of Teen Challenge. I was a complete wreck. I barely weighed 100 lbs, I was detoxing, I was angry, and I was definitely not a Christian. Those first few weeks were the most difficult. For the first time in almost nine years, I actually had to face all the terrible decisions I had made and the people I had hurt. And I had to do it sober. Because sleep was impossible, I would go down to prayer from ten to eleven every night, even though I wasn't a believer. It was just something to do. One night, a friend of mine asked if he could pray for me. It was at that moment Jesus spoke to my heart and revealed Himself to me. Right then and there I accepted the Lord. It was like a light switch was turned on. I went from always being angry, depressed, and full of anxiety to being happy, calm, and in a relationship with the Lord.

While in the program, I served on the Drug Awareness Team and in Program Development. As time progressed and my family saw how serious I was about my sobriety and my walk with the Lord, relationships began to heal and ultimately my family, friends, and loved ones were restored. Today I work with all of my uncles who welcomed me back with open arms and forgiving hearts. The Lord changed my heart and filled me with so much gratitude and it still carries with me today. Today I am confident, secure, loved, and accepted. I no longer have those voids inside my heart, and I no longer feel unworthy of God's love. I have seen so much favor in my life simply because I gave up doing things my way and decided to obey the Lord instead.

> Almost all of my court cases in Rhode Island and Connecticut were cleared up without jail time.

I graduated the program in September of 2013 and have never looked back towards my old life since. I am a changed life!

Neal & Kristy
I met Neal at a fundraising event the day before I

graduated the program. We briefly talked and I encouraged him to stay the course and wished him well. He said he knew that day that I was going to be his wife. About six months later the men's Teen Challenge choir came to my home church and I got to hear Neal's testimony for the first time. As I sat there and listened, I felt I was listening to my twin speak and could see such a change in him from the first time we had met. There was a visible difference in his countenance and I knew that Jesus had filled his life and changed him. We briefly spoke again and I knew that day that we were supposed to be connected.

After he completed the program, we started talking and dating. Our first date was serving the homeless together. We created such a beautiful bond that day using everything that we had been through in our lives with such purpose and zeal. We never questioned whether or not we should be together, we just knew that God had brought us together. We would often talk on the phone, sharing scriptures and encouragement with one another, building up our relationship in such a way that was so different from anything we had ever experienced before. Sending sermons and songs to each other became a part of our daily routine, and we never had to force anything in our blossoming relationship. It was so easy and so right, because God was in our midst. We had to learn what Christian dating looked like since we both had no idea.

Changed Lives

The evidence of our truly changed lives became evident when we fell into sexual sin. We instantly felt an extreme amount of conviction from the Holy Spirit and we both knew that the temptations that we faced outside of Teen Challenge were very real and powerful. A month later I found out I was pregnant and by God's grace, we were able to turn back to Him in our time of need. When we fell short we didn't stay stuck in it, we got right back up and continued to walk forward in forgiveness. We knew that we had to get married as soon as possible so we wouldn't fall into that sin pattern again. We both wholeheartedly wanted to serve the Lord and wanted our lives to reflect Him in every way. Our hearts turned towards the Lord and we saw His hand of favor on our lives as we honored Him first and foremost. We received godly counsel and began planning for our marriage. God opened many doors of blessings for us to have a marriage that was so intimate and sacred. We were married in July of 2014 and our son Caleb was born a short time after. Being a parent is one of the greatest privileges ever entrusted to us. We strive to allow him to live a fulfilling life, breaking the cycle of disaster and death that had been passed down through generations.

Today we are an active part of our church, serving together to help others find freedom from addiction and other life-controlling issues. I serve at the Teen Challenge Rhode Island Women's Home where I pour into the lives of broken women, and love them back to life. Neal is an industrial mechanic working with his family and is moving his way up in the company. My husband has become a leader not only in our household, but among our church community as well. We both have a passion for fitness and living a healthy lifestyle, and we enjoy outdoor activities such as fishing, canoeing, and hiking. We have plans of purchasing our first home in the near future. God has done so much in our lives both individually and as a family. We have seen the Lord's kindness and faithfulness in our marriage as we have been through many challenging seasons. He helps us to have a strong foundation in Him that has kept us aware of His wonderful promises for our lives. Today we are so hopeful for our future and we know that God provides for our every need according to His glorious riches. We have been shown a new way of living and God has helped us learn to place our trust completely and fully in Him. Our family is blessed by our changed lives! We want to leave you with one more thought: What God has done for us He wants to do for you too.

Chapter 9
I Am Not a Mistake

Gilles Gentley

Have you ever felt like your life was a mistake? Did you ever think that maybe even God was surprised by your birth? That you didn't have value or your life was an accident? Maybe you felt too stupid or just too limited to do what you thought you should. Well, if so, I know how you feel, because I felt all the same things in my life.

I grew up in Newport, Vermont, a small Canadian border town. My family is of Canadian descent. This meant two things for me: One, we were proud to be French, and two, we worked hard and played harder. My grandfather was a farmer. I remember as a kid spending long days on the farm driving a tractor and bringing in the hay with him. But I also watched him at the end of the night drink himself to sleep on the couch.

One day he decided that he was too old for farming

and sold the family farm. After that, he bought a convenience store which has both good and bad memories for me. For us, family was everything. I was told this all the time growing up and shown it too. This meant that we all worked at the store whenever we could. Just like the farming, we were there whenever the family needed help.

Telling you this now makes me feel like I am giving up family secrets, but I am not putting the blame for my problems on anyone. I'm only trying to share with you my mindset so that you can understand the choices I made a little better. My parents, products of the seventies and on the hippie side, used drugs every day. I don't ever remember a day in my life when drugs were not there. o.

One day my parents found a great little "babysitting" service that helped them on Sunday morning. It was a local church and a woman that drove the church van to pick us up for Sunday School and drop us off afterwards. We brought home papers and coloring sheets from the lessons. These papers became a witness to my mother and caused her to seek God. She went to this same little church and made a decision that changed everything: She accepted Jesus into her life and got saved! Her decision impacted our little family and caused a ripple effect that would last for years.

That encounter with Jesus changed her so much that she no longer wanted to get high or drunk. Instead of wanting to go to bars or to party at home, she now wanted to go to Bible study and church services. But not everyone thought that was so good. My father hated it and grew to resent her and God. Things turned bad pretty fast because of this and life in our family changed drastically. My parents divorced. It was a nasty split and things were done and said that were damaging and left scars for years.

It was during this time that something was said that impacted my life in a major way. I couldn't tell you right now what the fight was about or what was really going on. All I remember is my father was trying to hurt my mother through me. He was violent with my mother frequently, but this time he chose to use his words. He said to me, "You were a mistake. We never wanted you. We wanted to have an abortion. Yeah, that's right, go ask your Mom. She's so Christian, see what she says about that."

I can't explain how deeply that hurt me and the thoughts that went through my head. Those words haunted me for many years to come.

> I was a mistake, an accident, so unlovable that not even my parents wanted me.

From there on out this was how I looked at life. I am an accident so what difference does it make? I made bad choices because I thought, "what does it matter? After all, I am a mistake."

After my parents got divorced, I acted out at school, getting into fights and causing lots of trouble. A nice lady at church decided to make an investment in my brother and me, believing the Word of God would help us. I was ten and he was seven and we had seeds planted in our lives that would take years to harvest.

My mother brought my brother and me to Sunday school, church, and youth group. Newly single and raising two boys, she did what she knew. My mother is a brave and strong woman who taught me a lot. I wish I had listened to her warnings. My friends at this time were all at the Christian school or from youth group. I could speak "Christianese" and put on a good show, but I struggled with surrendering my life to Jesus. Why would I want to live for a God who saw me as a mistake?

After a few years I returned to public school and this is when things started to turn for me. My mom had remarried and my brother and I got a stepbrother and stepsister. Today they are family, not steps. Home life was crazy and it was easier to stay out with friends and get high than it was to go home and fight with my stepfather. He was a big man and drank a lot. He would get mad and take it out on me. This led me to stay away as much as I could.

Not being around my Christian school/youth group friends anymore, I quickly went back to smoking marijuana. It was almost like falling in love. I loved to drink beer and smoke pot. It made me one of the boys. It made me feel like I had never felt before. I was funnier, I had confidence, and people wanted to be around me. I still had the mindset that everyone did this and it was normal. I was consumed by this and it became my identity. Gilles the druggie, he knows where to score. My goal became how to do as many drugs as possible before I graduated. I thought that after graduation, I would go to college, stop using drugs, and have a good life.

Somehow I managed to graduate high school. That was a miracle! Really, the only reason that I did graduate was my pride. My freshman year a guidance counselor told me I was a loser and would never amount to anything. His advice was for me to quit school and get a job in the local mill, because that's all I would ever be. But I wanted to graduate to prove him and everyone else wrong.

After graduation I moved to Southern California. I wanted to get away from God and my family that was preaching to me all the time. I had enough of the God thing and wanted to get as far away from Him as possible. I had seen TV news and from what I could tell, God wasn't in Southern California, plus it was as far away as I could get within the states. I went there with the intent to go to college. In-state tuition was cheap, and my father lived there, so I figured I could use his address and get in. But the day I was supposed to go to take tests and register for classes I was late because I was buying drugs.

My early years of drugs included smoking pot, drinking beer, and occasionally using psychedelic drugs. That all changed once I got to California. I found harder drugs easier to get. My choices led me to become homeless. I only cared about one thing, and that was me.

> I was like the prodigal son. I felt like I was living in a foreign country, struggling to eat and survive.

But the Vermonter in me wouldn't give up. I would always work and do what I could to survive. I would bounce back, get a temp job, rent a hotel for a week at a time, and do what I could.

This became a cycle because of the choices I was making. I traded in a pot habit for a crystal meth habit. I could work long days, party, and go back to work. Sleep was sparse but I didn't need it because of the meth. I worked, stayed up five or six days, and then wanted to come down. To do this, I used heroin so I could sleep. A few days later I would do it all over again.

Somehow, in my madness, I was able to get an apartment. I worked hard and my life looked good to other people. I was still using like a madman but I was able to fake it. I looked good from the outside but I was a mess inside. I was able to have the apartment by having roommates. One of them was my brother and I dragged him into addiction with me. Kids from the area came to hang out at our place. There was always a party going on.

I seemed to have control of this work-and-party thing. It was a hard balance, but I was doing it. I remember one night my other roommate brought over some friends he knew from school, and he introduced me to a young lady who caught my eye. She and I started to see each other. We had many things in common and hit it off well.

One Saturday night she woke me up and said, "Let's go to the bedroom." I didn't have any objections to that. She wanted to talk, but I didn't. She told me, despite me trying to go back to sleep, that she was pregnant. My answer was simple: You need an abortion. I was an addict and was in no place to raise a child. It was here that I can say I saw my mother's prayers starting to take effect. There were a lot of things that happened that I don't have the time to write about in this one chapter, but the end result was that we decided to have the baby.

Nine months later I was the proud father of a beautiful baby girl. We named her Hannah and she changed my life and impacted me in so many ways. As much as I was in love with her and loved being a dad, I was still struggling with addiction. I was able to get myself off the hard stuff, but I was on what is called in recovery "the marijuana maintenance program."

Changed Lives

I'm just smoking pot, I told myself. I thought I wasn't hurting anyone.

At that time I lived in a rough area of California. Growing up in Vermont, I knew that there was a better place to raise kids, so three months later I moved my family across the country. Years prior, I left Vermont a single pothead kid out of high school. Now I was returning with a family and a heroin habit.

I worked a lot, and smoked, drank, and did whatever else I could. I was still able to act like an adult and hide my addiction for the most part. People knew that I liked to drink and smoke but never knew how bad it was. I worked as a tradesman and was able to put a roof over my family's head. I did the things I thought a good man was supposed to do. I was even able to play church and fool people about how well I was doing. I was living in the old Vermont, before heroin was everywhere and Rolling Stone magazine was doing articles on how bad the drug problem was there. These were the days when everyone in Vermont smoked pot, listened to Phish, and ate Ben & Jerry's ice cream.

That woman who was crazy enough to come to Vermont from California actually married me. I was trying my best to do right by her and my daughter. We had another baby girl, Aylina. She was such a gift to me from God, but I wasn't smart enough to see it. I managed to buy a house, have a wife and two daughters, and things were going better than I deserved, yet I was only focused on me.

We had been attending a church and I was really trying to get and stay clean. I could always string together a little clean time but could never maintain it. I found that Jesus was my celestial bellhop. When I needed Him I could call on Him and He would help me. But I still couldn't surrender my life to Him. Even though I recognized God's call on my life to be a pastor and was working in the church and taking classes towards my pastoral degree and thought this was it, I still hadn't fully surrendered my life.

I remember the day that things got really bad. I got a call at my work telling me that my stepbrother was hurt in a car accident. I drove to the hospital before he was airlifted to Dartmouth Hospital not knowing if I would ever see him again. A few weeks later he did come home in a back brace with a pocket full of pills. I had never heard of the pills, but he said they were good, so I tried one with him and I'll never forget that it was that old familiar high of heroin.

It began as a weekend thing. We partied and did a few pills, nothing much. It really wasn't a big deal because my brother's insurance was paying for the pills, and I didn't see the harm. We started taking them a little more frequently, during the weekdays, and using more pills each time. I really didn't think that I had a problem until his insurance company stopped paying for them. This meant that I had to start using heroin again. In Vermont, heroin was more difficult to get. I had to make trips to the city to get drugs and pay higher costs. I had to be creative as to how I was able to afford my drugs. It wasn't long before I was hooked more than ever before. I was also hiding it better, or so I thought.

I was able to keep it secret for a while, but my behavior and actions revealed what was going on.

I was completely backslidden from the Lord and completely addicted.

My family was begging for me to get help and get clean. I didn't want to hear that at all. My little house of cards was falling in around me. The house we had bought was in foreclosure. I was behind on payments and owing everyone money. My life was out of control and I was the last one to realize it.

One night I remember lying on my couch and detoxing badly. I promised my wife that I wasn't getting high anymore, but I was thinking of every excuse to get high. My wife said that if I got high again, she was done with me. I thought I could talk my way back in – I'd use guilt, anger, or something. So I went and got high. When I returned about three days later, she told me I wasn't good for her or my daughters and that I needed to go. She didn't care where but my time with her was up. She proved this by having my clothes already packed in trash bags for me. I didn't know where I was going to go. I needed time to figure things out.

I went to my mother's place. I knew that I could stay the night with her and figure out my next move. I was back in my childhood bedroom, getting high. I still thought my drugs were not hurting anyone, but then I thought of my girls, lying in bed that night crying over their drug addicted Daddy like they had so many nights before. I thought of my wife who was trying to stay strong as she figured out how she was going to survive the mess I had made. I thought, "I am a junkie, all I will ever be is a junkie, and I need to die a junkie's death." I knew I had enough drugs with me that I could commit suicide right there and it would look like an accidental overdose. I sat there crying and trying to talk myself into taking my own life.

Crying out to the God I was mad at and had abandoned, I yelled at Him and asked Him how He could let me get like this. In that moment I heard a voice audibly. God spoke to me and said, "Gilles, it's My grace and mercy that you're not in jail or dead." I knew He was right. I also had a sense of peace that I had never experienced. The next morning I called the pastor of the church I had once attended. He agreed to talk to me.

When we met, he told me I needed Teen Challenge. I told him that he must have been high because I knew that place and was not going to go there; that place was full of nuts!!! They had come to my church a few times. He convinced me to visit and talk to them. Things looked good, but I still hadn't bought in yet. On our ride home I was quiet, processing the whole thing. I still didn't believe my life could be saved. I didn't believe God wanted to save me or that He would even have anything to do with me. All of a sudden a song came on the radio by a popular artist and the chorus was "I'll take you back." Right there, God spoke to me and let me know that He would do something with my life.

On August 6, 2006, I went into Teen Challenge Vermont thinking I would do thirty days. I was going to use this to get sober and get back home. God had a different plan. Two weeks into the program, I remember the preacher talking and he couldn't stop talking fast enough for me to get to the altar. His message was called, "You must decide your moment of surrender." One of his points was that many are called but few are chosen. He went on to say that what it really meant was that few choose to be the chosen. I knew this was my day. I had been running from the call of God on my life and today was my day to surrender.

I remember thinking of all the times God saved my life, the times He tried to reach me and I was too prideful and stubborn.

When I could get to the altar, I made my peace with Jesus. I cried and told God that I was done. My life was a mess but if He wanted it, it was His. I finally surrendered my life to Jesus then and there and my life has not been the same since.

I can think of so many times and ways that God spoke to me and how He has changed me. One of the greatest times was one day in the Teen Challenge Learning Center. I was studying the Bible and there in Ephesians 2:10, God spoke to me. The verse says that before the foundations of the world God prepared good works for me to do. I'll never forget the first time I read that verse and how I felt. I wasn't a mistake, but God's masterpiece. It was like those verses were in neon flashing at me.

I did complete the program. My plan of thirty days went out the window. I also got divorced while in the program. But with God's grace, my relationship with my daughters and their mother improved. I was able to become the father that my children deserved. Completing the program was the hardest thing that I had ever done, but God was changing my life so much that I didn't care how hard it was. The cost was worth it. When I graduated, my life was so different that the only thing that made sense to me was for me to stay on and help others who were like me, stuck in addiction and not knowing there is a way out. So that is just what I did. I worked for Teen Challenge Vermont in many different capacities.

About year and a half after completing the program,

God heard my cry and He sent me a beautiful woman. This was my first hard test of obedience. There was a strict dating policy and before we could date, I had to introduce my date to my pastor. As hard as this was for me, it was also proof to me that she was the one. Who in their right mind, in their thirties, would meet someone's pastor and agree to follow the guidelines? The whole thing was difficult and humiliating, and it was the thing that blessed us more than anything. A year later I proposed to her and Sarah became my wife. God blessed me and my life was coming together. I had my daughters back in my life, and on top of that I gained two stepdaughters and two stepsons. Life was pretty good.

While I was serving at Teen Challenge Vermont in the Admissions Department, God humbled me in a good way and broke my heart. He enabled me to see men as He did. I loved the work I was doing. Along with working, I continued classes at night so that I could get my credentials and finally become a minister.

I did reach my goal. Since a young child, I knew that I was called to serve God full-time. I had been with Teen Challenge for ten years and felt that God had opened up the door in my life for me to fulfill my destiny. I became the associate pastor of a small church in Vermont and I served there for about one and a half years. I am so grateful for that church and the people I got to serve there. I was able to serve as a man of God with Rick Menard, like a son with his father. I was taught so much there that I can't write it all down in these pages. As much as I grew and learned, it became painfully evident that I was not where God had called me to be.

Pastor Rick Welch, who is my hero in life and in ministry, asked me if I could help him at Teen Challenge in Connecticut, so I returned and accepted the position of Assistant Director. Pastor Rick was the man who was there for me in my moment of desperation and helped me to change and grow. When he told me that he needed help, I proudly wanted to return the favor.

I am still pastoring people, yet not how I thought I would. Growing up, I thought all pastors had to have a church. They don't, only a flock. Today I am walking in the knowledge that I am God's masterpiece and doing what He called me to do. I am a father, a husband, a son, a brother, and a pastor, but most of all, a servant of Jesus Christ. I love every one of my titles, but the servant of Jesus is the most important one. It's because of Him that I have my life today and I want to spend it helping others to find their life in Him.

I want you to know that your life is designed by God. You are not an accident or a mistake. You are fearfully and wonderfully made by a God who loves you very much and wants to use you for His glory. Know that God created you for a purpose. Find Him and you will find your purpose.

Chapter 10
A Princess Warrior

Emma Martens

My life began in California as the firstborn of my parents who were finishing school and just getting started in life. I grew up in the church and learned about God and Jesus in Sunday School. I remember the leaders talking about His attributes, works, and that Jesus loved me. I learned the Bible stories and memorized many scripture verses. When I was four we moved to Texas and I attended a private Christian school. So as you can see, I grew up in a loving home that loved the Lord.

In the fourth grade I met a girl I allowed into my life as my first "best friend." She was a sweet girl for the first year. Her dad was a pastor and her mom worked for a Christian teen pregnancy agency. During fifth grade, however, my best friend shifted from a healthy, godly girl, to one of the meanest and most prideful ones I knew. This friend taught me how to lie to people, manipulate any guy into falling for me, and being the queen bee of the school. It was my first experience being friends with somebody whose values were so different from what I grew up with. But because of our friendship and "best friend" status of the previous year, I decided to keep her in my life and encourage her dangerous behavior, but I kept this side of her hidden from my parents.

On one of the last days of school that year, she came over to my house and told me that she recently had sex with her crush. I was so fearful for my friend; I didn't know how to react. For the first time, I turned to my mother and cried the story to her, not knowing what else I could do. I didn't know how to communicate my feelings and how to cope with "sex." My mom wrote an email to my friend's parents and I never saw her again. I felt so betrayed. Imagine practically living with someone for two years straight, we were "best friends," and then they were gone because you genuinely wanted to help them. Because I wasn't met with the emotional support I felt was appropriate, I decided that because I had tried to solve things with my parents and it ended with me losing my best friend, I would handle situations by myself in the future. I was puzzled, this girl had come from a Christian family and pretended to have a strong faith in front of others. Her actions caused me to start having some serious doubts about the Christian beliefs I grew up with and whether it was real at all. Reflecting on this friendship, I now see how Satan fed lies into my mind about what my worth and identity was.

Two years later, another significant event happened in my life. Every summer, my dad's side of the family gathered for a family reunion at a cabin in Canada. The trip up to Canada was always my favorite vacation. The views were so different than the flat land I was used to in Texas. My family members were sweet and excited to see me and it was the highlight of my summers. One year, however, things started shifting between my cousins and me. Because we were getting older, the overall mood and conversation among cousins began turning to more mature topics.

Over the course of the week while we were gathered in the cabin, one of my male cousins, two years older, molested me. I was confused and upset, so I turned to my closest female cousin and in a teary mess confessed the truth to her. She looked at me and said, "Emma, I'm sorry. I love you and you have never lied to me before, but I just can't believe that he would do that. He is not that kind of person and I can't see that happening."

Humiliated and not wishing to break the family up further I dismissed the topic altogether and assured myself I must have imagined it. I had grown up with him; I reasoned that he was incapable of committing such an evil.

In the back of my mind, however, the fear of communicating

pain and evil situations to someone and them not believing me continued to feed the lie that people, and parents, could not be trusted.

That same week a couple days later, while out on a boat with my two cousins, I saw him trying to do the same thing to her. Horror was stricken all over her face and it broke something in me. I turned to him demanding that we go back. Once home, my sweet cousin and I went to our room where she collapsed in my arms, overwhelmed by the reality that what I had been saying was the truth. When he had seen what happened, our male cousin apologized for what he had done to the utmost degree. After, though, he sent both of us texts about how it was our fault and we shouldn't be upset. He claimed he had done nothing wrong and that it was not a sin to be in a "physical, not sexual" relationship. He said we would even have a more connected bond. The next morning, my female cousin and I told our parents little about what had happened, but fearing that it would result in tearing our families apart, we didn't fully tell them every detail except that he had "tried" to touch us.

My parents handled things by having him repeatedly apologize for what he had done in front of our families and he couldn't be around us anymore, although the words fell on deaf ears. I had no reason to believe his words were anything more than a brief, insincere apology. I knew he would not put them into action and I wanted to be justified. I still didn't trust my parents enough to tell them about what had happened and Satan had my entire life wrapped around his lies after that. This trauma left me with built-up resentment towards my parents and an unhealthy view of myself. I now believed I was worthless and served no higher purpose than receiving sexual attention. During this time I remember continual arguing between my parents and me. I wanted so much to communicate and share my heart with them, yet instead I shut down my emotions and thoughts and kept a distance from them.

It was ultimately this nonexistent relationship with my parents that led to my downfall. I had no healthy example to talk to. Although my options were very open, I still struggled with sharing what happened to me with other people.

I was ashamed because I believed the situation was entirely my fault.

The manipulation and lies I was told became my reality because I thought I couldn't communicate what I was feeling or thinking to anyone.

Later that year, while attending my weekly Bible study, my friend and I were sitting in a room together talking. Suddenly, a group of five guys walked in and shut the door. They proceeded to make remarks about the fact that there was no camera in the room and the only window had been covered with black paper. The entire situation left me terrified and feeling weary. I felt powerless, the feeling of being abused raced back to my mind. I couldn't re-live what had happened to me before and grabbed my friend and we raced out of the room.

I was exposed to the world by a supposedly "Christian" girl, I was molested by my "Christian" cousin, and then I was assaulted by a group of boys at a Bible study. These three offenses left me feeling overwhelming resentment and anger towards a God who would allow such things to happen, especially by His own people.

My heart hardened and I decided to deal with all the stress and pressure alone. I didn't know if I could trust anyone. Over the course of the following year I began acting out for attention and eventually moved through three schools. I was in a broken and lonely place. It was one night, however, that I lost all hope for myself and gave up on the future God had in store for me by trying to end my life. I was two hours from succeeding.

My parents had no idea what was happening inside with me. After a day in the hospital, I was sent to a Children's Adolescent Psychiatric Center. There, I was exposed to more evil and unhealthy people than I had ever been in my life. The therapists at the treatment center recommended books on self-esteem and promoted medicines and aroma therapy to cope with my situation. In this broken place, I saw the most hopeless children I ever met. Something in my heart broke seeing how these boys and girls thought of themselves and what they had done because of things that had happened to them. Little did I know these memories were what would later inspire a passion for the recovery of other struggling people like myself.

My parents, realizing the depth of my brokenness, started searching for a facility that could potentially bring their daughter back into the light.

By God's grace, Bloom had an opening and they took me there the day after I was released.

It absolutely broke their hearts at the thought of sending their daughter away to live in a different state. We had never been separated for so long before. The idea initially terrified me and I could not think of a single reason why moving away for months would benefit me more than seeking counseling close to home. What I didn't know was how extremely blessed I was to get into one of the two short-term Teen Challenge programs for adolescent girls in the country.

Arriving at Bloom, I was met with more love and kindness than I ever expected. The women on staff cared about me in a way only possible through the love of Christ.

Changed Lives

Through the uncomfortable counseling and self-reflection I was finally able to see myself in a new light. Where I had always believed that I needed unhealthy relationships and attention to live, I now found myself staring in the mirror to see not a nobody, but a daughter of the King. After years of hatred, anger, and resentment, I finally laid my life down in a humble attempt to start over and cleanse my heart and soul of whom I once chose to be. The decision was not easy, but I was ready to change.

One of the hardest parts was choosing whether my pride was more important to me than a potential relationship with a loving, good, perfect Father. I chose the latter because I was exhausted from the constant fight. I knew all along that God existed, yet I never cared enough to try and foster a relationship with my Creator. This was a God who not only loved the potential I had to do things for Him, but who also loved me at my very worst.

Throughout my time at Bloom, I learned about who Christ said I was and the future He had for my life. I no longer saw myself as another individual floating through life with no solid purpose other than existing. I wasn't a victim anymore. I was put on earth to guide lost souls to Christ. Even after all the evil I have seen and experienced in my life, I want to share how God healed me to help others on their salvation walk. There is far too much that we are made to be and do for His kingdom than to simply sit around and live our lives the way we want to. God's plan is holy and designed to fit our lives perfectly.

Now that I am back home, I am excited to enter into a new chapter in life. Although the time back has included struggles and temptations, I am overwhelmingly thankful to the staff at Bloom for giving me the tools to navigate through my troubling times and engage in a healthy relationship with my God and the people that mean the most to me.

I have experienced many of the secular solutions to trauma: medicine, various types of therapy, and "coping skills." The one thing that worked for me was seeing my life through the truth of God's word. At Bloom, I was taught how to cope with my issues and feelings and how to overcome them. My name is Emma Martens and I am a firm believer in Christ and His gracious works in my life. I am the daughter of a King, a warrior princess, and I am fully loved and accepted by Jesus. Hallelujah.

A Parent's Perspective and what God has taught us
Kevin and Lucinda Martens

God used Teen Challenge Bloom to radically change our daughter. That statement is the conclusion of what has been the toughest three years in our parenting lives. Emma is our oldest child, a very talented and bright girl who fell victim to sin chasing the desires of the world. The details of her story aren't the focus of what I want to share, but rather what God has shown us about His love, grace, and forgiveness for His children.

As Christian parents, we were determined to make Christ the center of our home. From the music that played, the importance of Church, to the schools we chose for our children, we were intentional in placing the focus on Christ and His Kingdom and serving Him on a daily basis. When our daughter started to struggle, it was hard for us. I think part of us felt that if we did all the right things from an early age that our kids would be somewhat "resistant" to the temptations of sin and certainly learn to love and follow Christ as we had hoped they would. This belief we no longer hold. We are in a battle: an everyday constant struggle between Satan and his forces against the Biblical truth of who Christ is. This battle needs much more prayer and dependence on Him than anything we could shelter them from or provide. And we need to be on offense because Satan is relentless in his attacks. This is one of the principles we have learned through Emma's experience.

Watching her go from the innocence of her childhood to a struggling teenager was hard. The transition of shifting importance from "parents to peers" was tough, the other kids at school were mean and cliquey, and this really opened the door for her collapse. The daily stress she faced and having to have the "right" answers and comebacks to her friends was exhausting. We watched her have so many highs and lows that we never knew from day to day which mood she would be in when picking her up at school. Little by little she made compromises, tried being the nice kid, the mean kid, the funny kid, yet all led to the same loneliness and frustration. Ultimately, we withdrew her from school, brought her to a Christian counselor, and had her tested by a psychiatrist to see if there was something we were missing. "Completely normal," "she's an amazing kid" were the answers we received from them all, but we knew we were losing her. Boys came on the scene and the pressures of social media, iPhones, and constant texting led to more pain in her life.

The most difficult day in our lives was when she decided life wasn't worth living and overdosed on medication.

As her parents, we felt there was nothing more we could do. We had exhausted all forms of help and still our child seemed dead and empty inside. We had been praying for months for God to awaken her heart, but whenever we pressed in on spiritual matters, her responses were empty and cold. We were broken and in so much pain. But this was ground zero for what God had in store for her and this was when Teen

Changed Lives

Challenge Bloom came into our lives.

Sitting in the hospital while the psychiatrists and mental health staff were "helping" her revealed just how broken the secular world of psychiatry was. After five days of inpatient care and therapy, during our first big family meeting, they announced their big plan for her, a book called *10 Days to Self-esteem*. Our child didn't need more self-esteem, she needed Christ-esteem. They also wanted her on medications and suggested we place her in a residential facility. We started journaling, diving deeper into scripture, and fasting. Where should she go? How were we to help her? How can we take her home like this? We couldn't possibly monitor her every second. But God was good. Through a series of past friendships and circumstances, we were told of another family's daughter who went through Teen Challenge and had a radical change for God. From here God took over. We prayed God would make His path clear for us, that He would open the one door that we were supposed to go through and to firmly shut any other doors. The one door that opened was Bloom.

I remember dropping her off and how painful it was. She looked at us both and said, "You don't send away a child you love, you only send away kids if you don't." As hard as it was to hear that, we knew precisely the opposite was true and that it was because of our love for her that we were doing this. We knew God had opened this door and we were going to be obedient and trust in Him. We dropped her off, did the intake forms, prayed our goodbyes together, and left her in God's care, giving her back to the One who gave her to us in the beginning. Somehow, this was more peaceful than we were anticipating.

At Bloom she began the accelerated Teen Challenge program and was supported with loving ministers, house parents, and a spiritual counselor who reached her. These ladies were ferocious prayer warriors who daily went to battle on behalf of Emma. The accountability, structure, and unconditional love she received there was just what she needed. We watched as she slowly "bought in" to the rules and structure, learned her identity needed to be in Christ, established a solid Biblical foundation, and finally put it all into practice in her daily life. As parents, we were able to see a relationship and depth of love for God that we had never seen in her before and her personality and countenance softened.

You could literally see the difference just by looking at her. God is gracious to his children and He met Emma there and restored her as only He can do.

During this time God gave us several "anchor points" of truth that we relied on for reassurance that He was in control. We wrote them down and read them over and over to keep us focused and not allow Satan any room for doubt about why we brought her to Bloom and why we knew she needed to be there.

1) He trusts us with Emma. He blessed us with her as a child knowing that we were the parents that could care for her needs. She was not a mistake and we were her parents.

2) He is not finished with her and is calling out to her. Evidence for this was that He wouldn't let her remain in her sin/impurity, but instead allowed her sins to be exposed to force her to address them. He is a loving God.

3) The Holy Spirit, through many real objective moments, was guiding this process. The circumstances that happened when she was at "ground zero," to the events that opened the doors at Bloom, all point to an active God steering the direction for where He wanted her.

4) She doesn't have a psychiatric diagnosis (as evidenced by the testing and therapists that evaluated her); she has a sin issue in her heart. This battle is spiritual and must be fought with prayer and the Armor of God.

5) The Lord is speaking to her. During her time there, God impressed on our hearts that He was reaching in and speaking to her and this was confirmed separately in discussion with her Biblical counselor. He is in this and He alone is capable of the redemption she needs.

Emma's homecoming felt like we were the prodigal son's parents celebrating the missing piece in our family for the past four months. There were no promises or guarantees at all that this was how things would turn out and this has given us an even deeper appreciation to God for what He did for her. Is she perfect now? Of course not. In fact, there have been some really tough conversations and restrictions placed on her since she left. But we know our daughter is transformed – we see it in her life by how she manages failures by resting on her identity in Christ. Her core knowledge of the Bible is amazing and she regularly leads our family in devotions she learned while there. To God be the glory, for only He can take what was broken and create something beautiful in its place.

If you have a teenage daughter struggling with any of the same or similar issues that Emma had, please don't hesitate to call Bloom's admissions office and believe that she can blossom into who God intended for her to be as well.

Chapter 11
Second Chance

Joe Rand

It was September of 2013. I was sitting outside on the back porch of my wife's Grandmama's condo in North Carolina overlooking the Smoky Mountains. From the porch I could see a golf course tucked into the valleys of the mountains, and golfers moving along the fairways. The thick clouds for which the mountains were named pushed along the ridgeside. Inside, my family was setting the table for breakfast. With my family in tow, we had driven almost 800 miles the last two days to spend the week visiting family. It was a fun drive. Sitting there in that moment I knew I would never go back to the life I had lived and been delivered from. Just over a year earlier I graduated from Teen Challenge in Brockton Massachusetts, and although I had never wavered or doubted during the program, this was the moment I really knew for sure. I thanked the Lord for all He had done for me and headed inside to enjoy Grandmama's sausage and grits.

I was born on August 2, 1985 in Weymouth, Massachusetts, and I was the youngest of three children to my parents, Ed and Pat. My sister, brother, and I were born just over three years apart. The first home I remember was in Mansfield, Massachusetts but I did most of my growing up in Lakeville, Massachusetts where I still live today. My father was a loan officer for a bank and also served in the church faithfully. I remember many nights he was at elder's meetings and some Sunday mornings he would preach. Later on, after I went to Teen Challenge, he left his position at the bank and became a full time Associate Pastor. My mother was an at-home childcare provider for as long as I can remember. She was always around, kids were always around, and there was always something to do.

I had a very good childhood and all my needs were provided. My family attended all my football games and we had many family vacations that I look back on with fondness. Most of my time was spent playing sports, hanging out with the neighborhood kids, and being with family.

I attended a Christian school from second through eighth grade. It was a small school and everyone knew each other. I always liked school because it was a place where I could be around friends and socialize. Throughout grade school I maintained pretty good grades, yet in high school that changed when I became very disinterested in school. When I wasn't in school or with friends, I was playing sports. I played Pop Warner football with the kids in town. I always felt at a disadvantage at the beginning of the year because all of my other teammates already knew each other from their school. It was for this reason I left the Christian school to attend public high school.

As the summer before high school progressed, I was faced with a lot of decisions that would impact my life. I often think about what I would have said to my high school self if I had had the chance. The reality is, I had a lot of good people around me, yet I didn't heed any of the good and godly advice I received. I'm not so sure there was anything anyone could have told me then.

There was a perfect storm brewing in my life because I cared more than ever about what people thought and I wanted to be friends with everyone.

Because I grew up in the church, was taught the Word of God, and had godly people around me, I couldn't simply choose the lifestyle I wanted. First I had to reject my current beliefs and morals and then go in another direction. I began to see the Word of God as only a rulebook dictating how I should live my life. I felt this wasn't fair because all of my new friends were writing their own rulebooks on what they saw as

191

right or wrong, what they could do and couldn't do. I wanted to write my own rulebook too. I wanted to draw my own line in the sand on what I could and couldn't do and what was right or wrong in my own eyes. Looking back I realize that each time I did whatever I wanted I drew a new line in the sand to justify my actions. The grip of sin was pulling me down and I hadn't even picked up a drink or drug - yet.

No one in my family smoked. Actually nobody I knew smoked. The first time I was offered a cigarette at a party I wanted so badly to fit in with my new friends that I went along with it as if it wasn't my first time. As soon as nobody was looking I went behind the shed and threw up. Later I told them that my pack had run out and I bought my first pack that night. It was that same group of friends that offered me my first beer. I got drunk three times the first week. Sure I still had my Christian friends from church, but instead of confessing to them, I boasted. I thought I was the coolest guy in youth group. I found some like-minded guys that wanted to try the things I was doing and we started hanging out. One morning while at my house he asked me if I would ever smoke weed. I thought about where I had drawn my line in the sand and told him "No, never." He told me he had a blunt rolled in his car ready to go and by that afternoon I had smoked weed for the first time. My line in the sand had moved again.

During this time I started getting in more and more

trouble. When some things happened in the church youth group that the leadership didn't approve of, they decided to kick me and three other members out. We were given instructions to think and pray about our actions and schedule a meeting with the Pastor. The other three guys were upset but secretly I was kind of happy. I saw it as a way out. My parents had already been forcing me to go and if the church didn't want me to go, my parents couldn't make me. Eventually I was invited back even though I never met with the Pastor, but it was a new season of me pulling away from God, church, and godly influence.

I quickly began getting in trouble at school and my freshman year was a complete failure. I was so used to the Christian school with small classes and teachers who would hold you accountable for everything. It was different now. When my football season ended with an injury to the muscles in my neck, I lost all motivation. I was used to being made to stay awake and hand in all of my homework, and now I slept through algebra halfway through the year and then was switched to study hall because it was impossible for me to pass. Once I realized I never got in trouble for not handing in my biology lab work I stopped altogether. Halfway through the year, I had a low grade of 17 in the class. Barely passing any classes, after summer school, I had to go back to the Christian school, however, I didn't fare much better my sophomore year. Now I had had too much of a taste for the world outside. I don't remember exactly how many detentions I got that year, but I do know some were never recorded by teachers and the principal in an attempt to show me grace. By the end of that year it was obvious that I needed an alternative if I was going to make it through high school. That alternative was an online homeschool group. They sent me the books and materials to learn on my own and I had to mail in my answer books and tests. There was a lot of cheating to get by those last two years, something I am not proud of. I started working full time, which was a great way to get me out of the house and around more mature people. Unfortunately, the influx of money helped fuel my partying.

Trouble began catching up with me at home too. I was coming in late and rushing to my room to avoid conversations with my parents. I don't know exactly when they figured out I was drinking and smoking, but they started catching me with bottle caps, bags of weed, pipes, and other signs that I had strayed off course. The battle was only beginning. Looking back I can't believe the amount of love, grace, and patience they had with me – levels that only come from spending time before God in prayer. I believe there were many times God spared me during these reckless years and He already began answering the prayers of my parents.

> Pills started getting more popular my last couple years of high school, Oxycontin in particular. It was time for me to move my line again.

My introduction to Oxycontin changed my life. It was a high I had never experienced before and I loved it. It made all drugs seem like they were less than and gave me the boldness to try and do anything. And that is exactly what I did, everything. Life became a game of how many drugs I could get ahold of and how high I could stay. It was all I wanted to do and I saw nothing wrong with that.

As my life began to spin out of control, my parents gave me an ultimatum. They presented me with the opportunity to go away for the summer to a training program at a Christian campground in upstate New York or choose to be homeless. I was torn because I really did not want to leave for the summer but something inside of me knew I had to. My parents were in full desperation mode to get me out of my hometown. I was convinced I needed to stay and work to make money, so instead they offered to buy me the things I thought I needed if I would stick it out for the summer. Today I can only attribute my leaving for the summer to God working in my life and preparing me for the ministry He had for me in the future. If I hadn't left there was a good chance I could have slipped further away from God and the people I needed in my life. God got ahold of my heart again that summer and I was convicted of my sin for the first time since I had walked away from Him years earlier. In the bathroom of the dorm I stayed in that summer I recommitted my life to serving the Lord. That same day I destroyed all the drugs I had brought with me. Two things happened when I returned home at the end of the summer. I wish I could say that I kept my promises to the Lord, but I didn't. The first thing that happened was that I quickly realized that the group of friends I had been hanging out with had progressed into harder and more dangerous drugs, furthering my opinion that leaving may have saved my life. The other thing was that I joined back in. Rather than testifying to all the things God had done for me, I lied about my experiences and again, I denied God. But those next couple months were torture for me. I knew God had delivered me but I went back. By the time summer rolled around again, I knew what I needed to do. I went back for the summer training program. I had another awesome summer and I saw God work in my life and use me to minister to others. I decided to attend the Bible college that was affiliated with the training program. It was a one-year Bible college with concentrated studies on the Bible, including ministry opportunities. At that school, Word of Life Bible Institute, I learned the Word, grew deeper in my relationship with God, and learned how to live it out in a practical way. During that year God confirmed the call He had on my life to be in ministry. I knew He had given me a "second chance" and my line in the sand moved again, but this time to align with God's will and purpose.

When I graduated the Bible Institute, I briefly started an optional second year that is designed to train up Pastors and Missionaries. I also started dating a young lady I had met. From the outside everything was going great, but inside I was losing my balance. Everyone thought I was doing well because I was not drinking, drugging, or partying, but I was slipping back into another area of sin, sexual sin. The conviction was eating at me. I knew what I was doing was wrong, even though most of my 19-year-old peers were doing the same thing. I had no idea how to be in a God-honoring relationship with another Christian and I was much too extreme a person to be living a half-truth.

I completely imploded. I left school with no explanation to anyone except that I felt I was in over my head. I was in over my head, but not with the schoolwork, with sin. I even left my girlfriend with no explanation to her other than saying "get away from me before I bring you down too." I did not accidentally run into my old friends. I went and found them and I went as hard as I could for as long as I could.

I started drinking to numb the pain of my mistakes, using cocaine to stay awake, and using pills to come back down.

Changed Lives

I spiraled out of control and ended up getting arrested with a DWI charge. That was grace because there was no telling how much farther I would have fallen. As it was, the arrest cost me my license, which cost me my driving job, which cost me my apartment at my place of work, and of course all my savings went to court costs and a lawyer. The most pain it cost me was my relationship with God. I grew angry with God that I was back where I started and that He would allow me to fall so hard. I made a decision during that time that I would never tie my sobriety into my relationship with God, so that if I failed in one area of my life, the other would still be strong. I was tired of feeling like every time I stopped reading the Word, I would fall back into drugs or every time I fell back into drugs, that I would lose my communion with God.

I was determined to do it on my own now, even if I had to white-knuckle it. I decided I would use alcohol and weed to help me stay away from the harder drugs. I started saying no to friends that wanted to hang out. I moved back in with my parents and got a job doing maintenance at a grocery store close to their house that I could walk to when I didn't have a ride. I started saving money again and tried getting my life back on track. I was still angry with God and refused to pray or read the Word. I just went through the motions, day by day.

The one thing I looked forward to each day was seeing a co-worker who worked in the deli department. As we spent more time together we learned that we had a lot in common and our affection for each other grew. I quickly learned she was a Christian, so I shared with her some of my past struggles with drugs and where I stood in my relationship with God. She knew I was angry with God and offered me godly advice. We eventually started courting and getting more serious with each other.

On July 11, 2007, I married Jeanne Connell. We decided to marry despite what anybody else thought. My family thought we were making a mistake, our co-workers thought we were crazy, and many of my friends didn't find out for months. We eloped and got married before a Justice of the Peace and two of Jeanne's sisters. We were young and in love, willing to conquer anything that came our way together. Our love was sure and we would need that love in the future to help hold things together when it seemed like our marriage would be lost.

In May of 2008 we learned Jeanne was pregnant and Willow Rand was born on January 21, 2009. During the pregnancy I struggled to hold things together. I worked full time making good money and I started going out with friends a little more. My old lifestyle started creeping back in. My drinking and partying became harder and harder to control. Jeanne chalked up most of my out of control partying to "a young guy getting it out of his system who would settle down once the baby came."

I hung out with friends and drink or smoke weed while they did opiates. I even drove them a few times, but I had no interest in destroying my life again. I was tempted, but I was unwilling to pay the high price for the pills. One day while at work I hurt my back and the doctor prescribed Percocets. I went right through that prescription and before I knew it I did what I thought I would never do. I used heroin. The very first time I let a friend shoot it into my arm in my living room, while my daughter slept in the bedroom. When I woke up the next day I called that same friend and asked him to get me more. When he didn't respond fast enough, I found it myself. I didn't know how to shoot it so I tried to sniff it, but it didn't get me high enough, so I called him and had him walk me through how to shoot it. Within 24 hours of trying heroin for the first time, I was hooked. I could not control myself or my actions. I had no idea what I was getting myself into. The first time I tried to stop for a couple days I got really sick. It happened so fast, I didn't even realize I was sick from withdrawals, I thought I had the flu.

> Once again my life started to spiral downward. Every thought and decision centered upon drugs.

It was my first thought in the morning as I reached under my mattress to get my first shot to get out of bed, and it was my last thought at night as I planned and prepared to make sure my high wouldn't run out the next day. I did things I never thought I would do. I went places I never thought I would go with people I never thought I would be with. I put my family in danger and I drained all the money we had saved without my wife's knowledge. The lies got deeper and deeper. I played my wife against my parents and my parents against my wife, trying everything I could to keep my run going, but it would all come crashing down.

At the end of 2010 I was forced to come clean, first to Jeanne and then to my parents. I went to detox and then a program, but I wasn't ready. I got my hands on a phone and had a drug dealer meet me right in the driveway of the program. I brought the drugs in and got high that night. The next morning I was tested and kicked out of the program. Another quick trip to detox, but before I could even go back to work I picked back up again. I was told "relapse is a part of recovery" and to "keep coming" but I was hopeless. When I looked up at the devastation I caused in my life and my family, I thought for the first time in my life that I would be better off dead. I did something that I rarely did, I looked at myself in the mirror, and I did not recognize the person I saw. I was hopeless.

Finally, I agreed to enter the doors of Teen Challenge

Brockton. I knew the only way I was going was if I went while I was still high. I was so high that I don't remember arriving there.

The first month was the hardest thing I ever did. The first week I packed my things to leave many times, but each time someone was able to convince me to put my stuff back in the closet. I couldn't even face a day at a time; I was doing one hour at a time. Each day was tough as I battled in my mind to stay or go. Almost two months after being there, I was caught smoking a cigarette behind the thrift store. I had enough. I walked off the property, jumped on a train, and walked to my wife's apartment. I showed up on her doorstep unannounced on a Friday night. Needless to say, she had mixed emotions. I told her how awful Teen Challenge was and that I was ready to come home, but she was not ready (and didn't believe me) and said I could not live with her. The next morning I went back to Teen Challenge to pick up my things and I was given an opportunity that not many people get, I was given a "second chance." As great as that was, what God gave me was greater. He gave me a new perspective. I came back with the perspective that I was in Teen Challenge because I wanted to be and needed to be. No longer would I battle with staying or going. I made up my mind that I would fight through the program no matter what.

I started to surrender my heart fully to God and allowed

Him to have His way. I made a commitment to pray for my wife and daughter every night during the last hour of prayer and for nine straight months, I did. God truly transformed my heart which started showing in the way I carried myself and lived my life. I wanted nothing more than to please the Lord and put Him first in my life. Because of that, God started giving me awesome opportunities to share His love with other residents and people I met on the streets. One of my last days as a resident in the program I went to Gloucester, Massachusetts to raise funds and awareness. While I was there, God put it on my heart to share the Gospel with someone. He left in a hurry that day, but I felt good knowing I was obedient to the Lord. Months later that man approached two residents at that same location and shared a story with them of how I witnessed to him and he went home that day and gave his life to Jesus. I knew that day that God was going to use me in this ministry if I stayed obedient and looked for opportunities to serve.

My wife and I began praying about me staying on for an internship at Teen Challenge (now apprenticeship). The Lord spoke to me and confirmed to Jeanne to stay. It was critical for both of us to know we heard from God because the internship was very difficult and many times I wanted to quit. The pay was low and I had to live on campus away from my family for another six months. But through all that, I just looked for ways to serve. I never expected in November 2012, while beginning the Emerging Leaders Program, that I would be chosen as the Program Supervisor. I remember sitting with the then Director, Oscar Cruz, and asking him what I needed to do in this role. He told me to just keep doing what I was already doing.

> So that's what I did. I kept looking for ways to serve God by serving others.

Eventually, Oscar and I would have the same conversation when I was asked to be Assistant Director, then the Associate Director, and now by the grace of God, Director. Each time his response was the same, as was mine. I was determined each step of the way not to look for ways to elevate myself, but for ways to serve God by serving others. For that reason, I believe God has increased my influence so that I can serve Him and others more.

My marriage was restored during my time at Teen Challenge. This is such a blessing and has helped to increase my faith. It took a lot of time, work, and healing, but God was faithful to bring us through to the other side. Our marriage is stronger now than the day we married. Not only that, but God saw fit to increase our family. In 2015, my niece Reagan came to live with us full-time. God completed our little family and provided us a home to put our roots down.

All this is why the family vacation to North Carolina was

so special to me. There were times in my life that I walked with the Lord and there were times that I was so far from Him. Yet when I graduated Teen Challenge in 2012, I could look back and see all the times when I fell away, the God of the "second chance" brought me back by His amazing grace. I can also see how the thing that Satan intended to destroy me was the very thing that forced me back down on my knees in surrender to God. Everything was brought full circle and all of the experiences in my life are now being used to bring glory to God and others into His Kingdom. One thing about the Lord is, what He does for one, He will do for anyone. Come to Jesus, surrender all, and you'll be amazed at how He will change your life too!

Chapter 12
Death by Fentanyl

Pasco A. Manzo, MACM

One of the first things I had to address as President of Teen Challenge New England & New Jersey was an ongoing lawsuit resulting from the overdose death of one of our Brockton, Massachusetts's residents who ingested a doctor-prescribed Fentanyl (Pronounced fen' ta nil) Transdermal Patch.

This is his story. He fell ill one night with what was thought to be bronchitis and was brought to the local emergency room. Upon examination, the doctor noticed he had chemical burns on his arms, which were suspected to be a result of some tire rim cleaner that he had used days earlier. This same chemical may have caused the inflammation in his throat, rather than bronchitis. The emergency room doctor was made aware that he had a history of drug addiction and was in a residential program getting help. Although the doctor suspected the resident was "drug seeking," he sent him home with a 72-hour Fentanyl Transdermal Patch. The two Teen Challenge staff that accompanied the resident had no reason to question or doubt the doctor's decision and they all returned to the center thinking the resident was going to be fine.

The next morning the resident was not up at wake up time, so a staff member went in to check on him only to find that, tragically, he passed away during the night in his sleep. Immediately, a staff member placed a 911 call. The medical examiner stated the cause of death as acute fentanyl toxicity. The resident had ingested the patch to get high sometime during the night and regrettably lost his life.

This was my introduction to this synthetic drug I learned was 50 times more powerful than heroin. I had no idea that in the days to come the word fentanyl would come up again and again as it would demand the lives of countless people who would overdose and breathe their last breath.

The following information is some of what I have learned. I am by no means claiming to be an expert on the subject nor am I giving advice. Most doctors and prescription instructions will tell you: "Fentanyl Transdermal Patches may be habit forming, especially with prolonged use. Use the fentanyl patch exactly as directed. Do not apply more patches, apply the patches more often, or use the patches in a different way than prescribed by your doctor. While using fentanyl patches, discuss with your health care provider your pain treatment goals, length of treatment, and other ways to manage your pain. Tell your doctor if you or anyone in your family drinks or has ever drunk large amounts of alcohol, uses or has ever used street drugs, or has overused prescription medications, or if you have or have ever had depression or another mental illness. There is a greater risk if you overuse fentanyl patches if you have or have ever had any of these conditions. Talk to your health care provider immediately and ask for guidance if you think that you have an opioid addiction or call the U.S. Substance Abuse and Mental Health Services Administration (SAMHSA) National Helpline at 1-800-662-HELP."

It has always amazed me when drugs and medication are administered to help one's ailment, sickness, or disease that they come with many potential and serious side effects. Regarding Fentanyl patches, the directions or caution says,

"Fentanyl patches may cause serious or life-threatening breathing problems, especially during the first 24 to 72 hours of your treatment and any time your dose is increased."

"Life-threatening breathing problems;" I am not a physician, but should we ever put anyone at this level of risk? "Your doctor will monitor you carefully during your treatment. Because of this serious risk, fentanyl patches should only be used to treat people who are tolerant (accustomed to the effects of the medication) of opioid medications because they have taken this type of medication for at least one week and should not be used to treat mild or moderate pain, short-term pain, pain after an operation or medical or dental procedure, or pain that can be controlled by medication that is taken as needed."

I offer this information, because we all need to know that Fentanyl is a very powerful synthetic opioid analgesic. It is a schedule II drug that is similar to morphine, yet it is 100 times more potent. **So potent that just three grains are lethal to an adult.** Yes, I repeat, so potent that just three grains are lethal to an adult. Fentanyl was first synthesized in the 1960's and has been used to treat patients suffering from cancer, severe pain of any kind, or to manage pain after a surgery. It has also been used to treat patients with chronic pain who have become physically tolerant to other opioids because of excessive use.

It appears that in today's society pain is the new four-letter word. People avoid it like the plague. Have we forgotten that pain can be a good thing? We learn, grow, change, and gain from pain. It acts as an alert for us to avoid harm or detect disease. We all experience pain at one time or another and people have different levels of pain tolerance, so for those who physically suffer continually, my heart goes out to you. As well as to those with emotional anguish and pain that brings despair. Thank God for His comfort and the comfort of our loved ones during these times. Yet may I suggest many would do well to consider pushing through their pain? Can we consider doing without addictive painkillers and using something over-the-counter to help ourselves and others avoid the additional problem of acquiring an addiction? Would the medical community consider this as well, and when called upon for help consider alternatives to alleviate pain as much as they can for their patients? Because for some "painkillers" are becoming just that, "killers."

I understand why dentists do not make it to the top of the list of most likeable people. I remember when I had to get my wisdom teeth removed. I wasn't looking forward to it, nor was I in a cheerful mood. My dentist gave me a prescription for Vicodin to ease the pain. I knew once I left his office and the anesthesia eventually wore off I may have needed it, but I chose to not fill the prescription at the drugstore. When I got home I took a couple of Aleve instead and they worked just fine.

In its prescription form fentanyl is known by such names as Actiq, Duragresic, and Sublimaze. Medically, fentanyl is used by injection, as a patch on the skin, as a nasal spray, or in the mouth. When producing the fentanyl patch perhaps they never gave thought that addicts would ingest them or melt them down and use a syringe to shoot it into their veins as they do. Street names for fentanyl or fentanyl-laced heroin include Apache, China Girl, China White, Dance Fever, Friend, Goodfella, Jackpot, Murder 8, TNT, Tanglo, and Cash.

As a controlled substance fentanyl is a high risk for addiction and dependence. It can cause respiratory distress and death when taken in high doses or when combined with other substances, especially alcohol.

Today the two main sources of fentanyl are the prescription drug industry and drug cartels. Fentanyl works primarily by activating u-opioid receptors.

Fentanyl is the culprit behind the current heroin overdose crisis, one of the deadliest drug epidemics in American history.

Fentanyl can also be made illegally and used as a recreational drug, often mixed with heroin or cocaine. Common side effects include vomiting, constipation, sedation, confusion, hallucinations, and injuries related to poor coordination. More serious side effects include decreased breathing, serotonin syndrome, low blood pressure, addiction, and/or even death. As of 2017, fentanyl was the most widely used synthetic opioid in medicine. Coincidentally the sharpest increase among overdose deaths from the years 2000 - 2016 were fentanyl related.

Drugs Involved in U.S. Overdose Deaths, 2000 to 2016

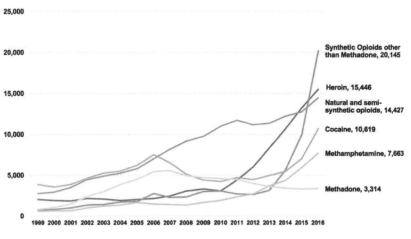

-National Institute on Drug Abuse

Similar to other opioids, fentanyl withdrawals can include: aches, adnominal cramps, anxiety, chills, cognitive issues, coughing, cravings, diarrhea, exhaustion, fever, goose bumps, insomnia, irritation, loss of memory, mood swings, nausea, pain, restlessness, running nose, sweating, watery eyes, weakness, vomiting, and yawning. People going through withdrawal often experience what can feel like depression or a void of feelings as well. This can last longer than many of the other side effects of withdrawal from fentanyl.

Now in the midst of this opioid crisis, many are asking "How did this happen?" In the late 90's, pharmaceutical companies reassured the medical community that patients would not become addicted to prescription opioid pain relievers such as Oxicontin. Healthcare providers began prescribing pain medications at greater rates, subsequently leading to widespread diversion and misuse of these medications. It didn't take long before it was clear that these medications could indeed be highly addictive. Opioid overdoses increased and have continued to increase since. According to Josh Katz from The New York Times, fentanyl deaths in 2016 were up 540 percent in three years.

The Surgeon General, Vivek Murthy, reported in 2017 that 1 in 7 people in the United States would suffer from substance addiction related to prescription or street opioid pain relievers. Only 10 percent of those addicted will receive treatment. Every 19 minutes an American dies from opioid or heroin overdose. The economic impact of drug and alcohol misuse and addiction amounts to $442 billion each year topping diabetes at $245 billion. According to the Center for Behavioral Health Statistics and Quality, 591,000 suffered from a heroin use disorder. In 2016 America lost more people to overdose opioid deaths (64,000) than we lost in the 19½ years of the Vietnam War. (58,148)

Here is what we know about the opioid crisis:
- It is estimated that 21 to 29 percent of patients who are prescribed opioids for chronic pain misuse

them.

- Between 8 and 12 percent develop an opioid use disorder.
- 27 million people self-reported misuse of prescription and illegal drugs.
- An estimated 4 to 6 percent who misuse prescription opioids transition to heroin.
- About 80 percent of people who use heroin first misused prescription opioids.
- 67 percent of families in the United States are struggling with active addiction.
- Opioid overdoses increased 30 percent from July 2016 through September 2017 in 52 areas in 45 of the 50 states.
- The Midwestern region saw opioid overdoses increase 70 percent from July 2016 through September 2017.
- Opioid overdoses in large cities increased by 54 percent in 16 states.
- 27,000 lives were saved as the result of Narcan kits given to friends and family to reverse deadly opioid overdose.

This opioid issue has become a public health crisis with devastating consequences across the entire United States. The epidemic affects most of us one way or another if not directly, then indirectly with increases in opioid misuses and related overdoses, rising incidences of neonatal abstinence syndrome because of opioid use and misuse during pregnancy, and children flooding the foster systems or having to live with grandparents or other family members because of their parents' opioid abuse. Fentanyl is playing a major role in the opioid crisis although available by prescription; it is the illicitly manufactured versions that have been largely responsible for the increase of overdose deaths related to synthetic opioids. Research shows that the increasing availability of illicitly manufactured fentanyl closely parallels the increase in synthetic opioid overdose deaths in the United States. (WebMD)

Today, drug dealers are adding fentanyl to heroin because it creates an intense high, which makes users feel drowsy, nauseated, and confused, but also euphoric. Dr. J.P. Abenstein, president of the American Society of Anesthesiologists, says the euphoria probably hits a lot faster when fentanyl is mixed with heroin and it's that super-quick potency of fentanyl that makes it dangerous; a little can go a long way.

Abenstein explains, "What happens is that people stop breathing on it, the more narcotic you take, the less your body has an urge to breathe.

And it makes sense that a lot of people are overdosing on it because they aren't sure how much to take."

Their brain is flooded with dopamine as the drug binds to their opioid receptors, and it activates their brain's reward centers. This creates a euphoric rush. The brain then wants to continue seeking whatever it is that created this feeling, so there is in a sense positive reinforcement to continue using and abusing the drug. As this goes on, a person will build what's called a tolerance to the drug. When this happens, there is the need to take increased fentanyl doses to get the same effect. This is incredibly dangerous with any drug but in particular, fentanyl, and as I mentioned already, it can be 100 times more powerful than morphine.

There are cases being reported that when heroin is laced with fentanyl, because of its potency and fast-acting effect, that even before the needle is taken out of the users vein they have overdosed.

First, fentanyl was found in heroin then it started showing up in cocaine. Next, they found it in counterfeit pills sold on the street – pills made to look like a sedative or opiate painkiller but consisting entirely of fentanyl. Now, it is marijuana that is being laced or sprinkled with fentanyl and even though no one has ever overdosed from smoking marijuana that will probably soon change.

Recently, a high school girl ended up in the hospital

after smoking marijuana with her friends. She reportedly took two hits off a joint, causing her chest and throat to start "burning." Her friends took her to get something to drink at a corner store, believing that she was dehydrated. When she started vomiting and began to black out, her "friends" took her to the woods and left her there. The girl's mother said: "I don't know if she had a guardian angel, but she was able to text a friend who was able to determine she needed help. I didn't even know if she was going to be alive when I got there." The good news is that, in this case, the girl was able to get to the hospital in time and was given a dose of naloxone to counter the overdose. The scary news is that there is no way to know when this will happen again or if the person involved will be enough to survive.

Fentanyl as a synthetic opiate is quite different than the version of the substance found on the street. It is very different from the medical grade fentanyl often given to patients in the hospital. In fact, it is so powerful that first responders and those who handle it must wear protective gear to avoid exposure. It is a threat to public safety. It only takes a very small amount of fentanyl or its derivatives, which can be inhaled or absorbed through the skin or mucus membranes (such as being inhaled through the nose or mouth), to result in severe adverse reactions, even life-threatening overdose. As a consequence, not only are users exposed to danger, but also so are others who encounter them including the general public, first responders, and law enforcement.

While writing this chapter, on June 26, 2018 an article was written by Amanda Milkovits, a Providence Journal staff writer.

She reported there was $1 million worth of fentanyl seized in a drug-trafficking bust in Providence, Rhode Island, in which three people were charged.

"Two Providence men and a Dominican national are accused of trafficking large amounts of fentanyl from Providence into Massachusetts and are facing federal drug charges. Providence police and agents in the U.S. Drug Enforcement Administration said they seized a total of four kilos of fentanyl. Sgt. Nicholas Ludovici, head of the Providence police intelligence unit, said the street value of the fentanyl was valued at more than $1 million. Providence has become a hub for heroin and fentanyl trafficking, as drug dealers move large quantities from the city into other cities in Massachusetts. During the three-week investigation, the police set up an undercover sting by arranging to buy three kilos of fentanyl and to meet at the Red Roof Hotel in Woburn, Massachusetts. The three were charged in federal court in Boston, Massachusetts with conspiracy to distribute and possession with intent to distribute 400 grams or more of fentanyl. If convicted, they face a sentence of 10 years to life in federal prison, and a $10 million fine. The Dominican man will face deportation proceedings after completing a sentence."

This is one operation that is now shut down because of the good work of the Providence police and agents and the U.S. Drug Enforcement Administration, but countless other traffickers are still out there killing our loved ones. Fight back by writing your congressmen and senators, and petitioning heaven.

Teen Challenge has been responding to the drug and alcohol crisis for 60 years. Starting in Brooklyn, New York with its first long-term residential center, it has grown to 261 centers throughout the United States and over 1400 centers throughout the world. On average in the United States there are 5,826 residents made up of men, women, and teenagers who are sleeping in one of our beds, overcoming addiction, and receiving the needed help and hope through our dedicated staff and the power of Jesus Christ. In 2016 it is recorded that 1,380,814 people young and old were contacted in outreach settings by Teen Challenge staff and our residents bringing a message of prevention and awareness.

Teen Challenge New England & New Jersey is committed to seeing every addict who comes through our doors be set free from the power of addiction. If the Son (Jesus) sets you free, you will be free indeed." John 8:36 We believe even in the midst of this opioid fentanyl epidemic that is claiming lives daily there is a greater power. "The One who is in you is more powerful than the one who is in the world." I John 4:4 That power is Jesus who can save and change lives to live free from addiction and reenter society with the tools and mindset to become a new person who is productive in every way. "Therefore, if anyone is in Christ, the new creation has come. The old has gone, the new is here!" II Corinthians 5:17

Death comes by fentanyl, but life comes through Jesus Christ. The battle for the addict is a daily tug-of-war … only prayer will prevail!

Teen Challenge New England & New Jersey's *End Addiction Campaign* team will bring their substance abuse prevention presentation to your school, youth group, or community event. It is interactive, multimedia, and includes real stories of people from all walks of life who have overcome addiction.

If you would like to schedule one of our End Addiction Teams to come to your community, please contact: endaddiction@tcnewengland.org

"It is easier to build strong children than to repair broken men."
— Frederick Douglass

Our *End Addiction Billboard Campaign* is an initiative to spread HOPE in our communities. **Help combat addiction by donating today!**

$850 will launch a 10'5 " x 22'8 " billboard for 4 weeks
$1,750 will launch a 10'5 " x 22'8 " billboard for 8 weeks
$2,750 will launch a 14 ' x 48 ' digital billboard along a major highway for 4 weeks
$5,550 will launch a 14 ' x 48 ' digital billboard along a major highway for 8 weeks

If you or someone you know is struggling, don't give up - change is possible!
Call the HOPE LINE today **1-855-404-HOPE**

Dollar-A-Day
Resident Sponsorship
Program

An Investment in Lives that Pays
Eternal Dividends

As a sponsor, you can be a lifeline of encouragement and support to an addicted person who is discovering God's love and a new life at Teen Challenge.

For just $1 a day/$30 a month, you can help underwrite the cost of a resident in the Teen Challenge program and give a man, a woman, or a teenager in our homes real hope for a promising future without drug or alcohol addiction!

Your partnership will be a tremendous encouragement to them as they are changed by a loving God from the inside out and become loving, healthy members of their families and a credit to their communities as caring, responsible, and productive citizens without dependence on drugs or alcohol.

Call **508-408-4378**
to see how you can become a Resident Sponsor!

Or visit our website: **www.tcnewengland.org**
to pledge your support.

Thank you!

223

CHANGED LIVES

Ten True Stories: *From Addiction to Freedom*

CHANGED LIVES books series is a compilation of miraculous stories of people who were addicted to drugs and alcohol and with no hope. But now through an encounter with God and the Teen Challenge Program, their lives have been changed. Is there a power stronger than the power of addiction? Can you or your loved one become FREE from the control of addiction and live a productive life? Absolutely yes! These books are a must read, the true stories will touch your heart, and give you and your loved ones HOPE!

Book 1

Book 2

Book 3

Book 4

Book 5

Single Copy - $15
Any Two Books - $25
Case (34-36 books) - Free Shipping - $350
Get yours today at: www.tcnewengland.org

Book Six Coming Fall 2019

TEEN CHALLENGE

COFFEE FOR CHANGE

**CHANGING LIVES
ONE CUP AT A TIME**

Our Products Include:

Ground
Whole Bean
Keurig Cups
Dark Roast
Decaf
Bulk 5 lb. bags

All Products $10.00

**Coffee Mugs
$5.00**

Tea Challenge

Our Products Include:

English Breakfast
Green Tea
Peach Apricot

All Products $10.00

**Tea Mugs
$5.00**

Visit our website **www.tcnewengland.org**
and find out about our bulk pricing!

Papa Pasquale's Sauce for Change

Our Flavors Include:
Alfredo Parmesan Cream Sauce
Carbonara Sorrento Sauce
Creamy Suga Rosa
Sunday Gravy
Pizza Sauce
Pomodoro Basil Sauce

Help change lives one jar at a time.

This authentic Italian product has been passed down from Pasquale's family's passion for delicious food, which began in the small mountain village of Cicerale in the Campania region of southwestern, Italy.

All Products $10.00 each
Case of 12 for $100.00

The land produced plants bearing seed and God saw that it was good.

Genesis 1:12

Book Teen Challenge

Church - Men's, Women's, and/or Youth Groups

Church presentations including testimonies, singing, program information, and product sales.

Community Drug Awareness Events

Table with addiction information, residents and staff to answer questions.

Social Clubs

Kiwanis, Rotary, and/or Lions

We want to be involved in your community

Contact the Teen Challenge Campus nearest you today!

TEEN CHALLENGE
Vehicle Donation

HELP CHANGE A LIFE AND DONATE YOUR VEHICLE TO TEEN CHALLENGE!

Every car, truck, mini-van, boat, and motorcycle
we receive helps fund the life-changing program of Teen Challenge!

Donating your vehicle to Teen Challenge is simple.
Visit www.tcnewengland.org or call 508-408-4378!

Teen Challenge Services

Maintenance

Brockton, Massachusetts
508-586-1494

Boston, Massachusetts
617-777-1193

Connecticut
203-789-6172

New Jersey
973-374-2206

Vermont
802-635-7807

Landscaping

Connecticut
203-789-6172

Maine
207-377-2801

New Hampshire
508-901-0168

Vermont
802-635-7807

Mechanic Shop

Brockton, Massachusetts
508-586-1494

Thrift Store

Connecticut
203-789-6172

Catering Services

Brockton, Massachusetts
508-586-1494

New Hampshire
203-668-8381

Jewelry

Rhode Island
401-467-0970

Snow Removal

Vermont
802-635-7807

Teen Challenge New England, Inc.

Teen Challenge New England is pleased to announce their new home for girls age 12-17 is open in Southern Massachusetts.

This short-term, 3-5 month program is helping girls struggling with drugs, alcohol, sexual exploitation, self-mutilation and more, discover their identity in Christ!

If you or someone you know is struggling with one of these issues, Teen Challenge and Bloom is here to help.
Call 774-300-8070 to speak to someone today.

Adopt a Bear!

Bloom Shirts

Ladies Guild

Every time you see this adorable bear, say
a prayer for the girls at Bloom or for a
loved one who needs help and hope!

Help change a life by sponsoring a student through our Dollar a Day program, joining our Bloom Ladies Guild, adopting a Prayer Bear, purchasing Bloom products and praying for each girl that enters our home!

Visit www.tcnebloom.org to learn more about our program for adolescent girls!

Vermont Women's Home

Coming Soon!

With drug overdose on the rise and the sexual exploitation of women, Teen Challenge New England & New Jersey, Inc. is excited to announce the opening of the first Vermont Women's Home that will address addiction and sex trafficking. Vermont has a great need for a women's long-term residential program since 41% of those seeking help in Vermont alone are women, and this type of care has been on the decline.

This home will also serve New Hampshire and Maine women.

For more information visit tcvermontwomen.org

Teen Challenge New England & New Jersey Headquarters and Short-Term Program

Coming Soon!

We have found that a hindrance for many is committing to a long-term (15-month) program. The short-term residents will intermingle with those who are in our long-term program. They will be able to attend chapel services, eat meals, receive group counseling, as well as spend recreational time together. We believe that when they see the transformation in our long-term residents' lives and their restoration with their families, 50 to 70 percent of the short-term residents will be encouraged to want the same.

This facility will have the potential to help up to
432 residents a year!

LOCATIONS

RHODE ISLAND WOMEN'S CENTER
572 ELMWOOD AVENUE PROVIDENCE, RI 02907
P: 401-467-2970
F: 401-461-3510
DIRECTOR@TCRHODEISLAND.ORG
TCRHODEISLAND.ORG

VERMONT WOMEN'S CENTER
130 HIGHLAND AVENUE HARWICK, VT 05843
P: 802-635-7807
F: 802-635-7029
DIRECTOR@TCVERMONT.ORG
TCVERMONTWOMEN.ORG

BLOOM ADOLESCENT GIRLS' HOME
P.O. BOX 603 BUZZARDS BAY, MA 02532
P: 774-300-8070
DIRECTOR@TCNEBLOOM.ORG
TCNEBLOOM.ORG

FUTURE NEW JERSEY WOMEN'S CENTER
SOUTHERN NEW JERSEY
P: 973-374-2206
F: 973-374-5866
DIRECTOR@TCNEWJERSEYWOMEN.ORG
TCNEWJERSEYWOMEN.ORG

BOSTON MEN'S CENTER
16 BLOOMFIELD STREET DORCHESTER, MA 02124
P: 617-318-1380
F: 617-318-1385
DIRECTOR@TCBOSTON.ORG
TCBOSTON.ORG

NEW HAMPSHIRE MEN'S CENTER
147 LAUREL STREET MANCHESTER, NH 03103
P: 603-647-7770
F: 603-647-7570
DIRECTOR@TCNEWHAMPSHIRE.ORG
TCNEWHAMPSHIRE.ORG

BROCKTON MEN'S CENTER
1315 MAIN STREET BROCKTON, MA 02301
P: 508-586-1494
F: 508-586-0667
DIRECTOR@TCBROCKTON.ORG
TCBROCKTON.ORG

NEW JERSEY MEN'S CENTER
245 STANTON MOUNTAIN ROAD LEBANON, NJ 08838
P: 973-374-2206
F: 973-374-5866
DIRECTOR@TCNEWJERSEY.ORG
TCNEWJERSEY.ORG

CONNECTICUT MEN'S CENTER
P.O. BOX 9492 NEW HAVEN, CT 06534
P: 203-789-6172
F: 203-789-1127
DIRECTOR@TCCONNECTICUT.ORG
TCCONNECTICUT.ORG

MAINE MEN'S CENTER
11 HUDSON LANE WINTHROP, ME 04364
P: 207-377-2801
F: 207-377-2806
DIRECTOR@TCMAINE.ORG
TCMAINE.ORG

VERMONT MEN'S CENTER
1296 COLLINS HILL ROAD JOHNSON, VT 05656
P: 802-635-7807
F: 802-635-7029
DIRECTOR@TCVERMONT.ORG
TCVERMONT.ORG

Do you have freedom?

Those struggling with drug and alcohol addiction are not free and desperately need the help of Jesus to save them, free them, and restore them! If you don't know Jesus, you too, need the freedom from sin and its weight.

Why do I need to know Jesus?

God created us to be in relationship with Him. Adam and Eve enjoyed a beautiful closeness with their Creator, but something tragic happened. They chose to disobey and rebel against God. This caused separation between God and man. All have sinned and fall short of the glory of God (Romans 3:23).

What does this mean for me?

God loves us so much that He sent His son, Jesus, to live a sinless life on earth, and then to die as a sacrifice for the sin that we deserve punishment for. Now our hearts can be made new and we can be reconciled back into a right relationship with God. This is Good News! Will you accept this free gift of salvation from your Father who loves you unrelentingly? (Romans 6:23) (John 3:16)

Where do I go from here?

To heaven when your life is over! Until then, walk with God, turn from sin, read the Bible, get involved in church, talk with God regularly, and tell people about this great news in your life.

"For Christ also suffered once for sins, the righteous for the unrighteous, that He might bring us to God." - 1 Peter 3:18 [ESV]